THE FIVE LOVE LANGUAGES

LANGUAGES

·······························

singles edition

THE FIVE LOVE LANGUAGES

singles edition

gary chapman

NORTHFIELD PUBLISHING

CHICAGO

Portions of chapter 11 originally appeared in *Dr. Gary Chapman on The Marriage You Always Wanted* (Chicago: Moody, 2005), 15–17.

All Scripture quotations, unless otherwise indicated, are taken from the Holy Bible, New International Version®. NIV®. Copyright © 1973, 1978, 1984 by International Bible Society. Used by permission of Zondervan Publishing House. All rights reserved.

Scripture quotations marked NKJV are taken from the New King James Version. Copyright © 1982, 1992 by Thomas Nelson, Inc. Used by permission. All rights reserved.

Editor: Randall J. Payleitner and Jim Vincent
Study guide by: Dillon Burroughs
Interior Design: Smartt Guys design
Cover Design: The DesignWorks Group Inc.
Cover Images: Heart Coffee Foam—Corbis; Coffee Mug—iStockphoto
Author Photo: David Smith

All Web sites and phone numbers listed herein are accurate at the time of publication but may change in the future or cease to exist. The listing of Web site references and resources does not imply publisher endorsement of the site's entire contents.

Library of Congress Cataloging-in-Publication Data

Chapman, Gary D.
        The five love languages singles edition / by Gary Chapman.
            p. cm.
        ISBN 978-1-881273-87-5
            1. Single people—Religious life. 2. Love—Religious aspects—
    Christianity. I. Title.

BV4596.S5C46 2004
248.8'4—dc22
                                    2004006514

This book is printed on acid free recycled paper containing 30% PCW (Post Consumer Waste) and manufactured in the United States of America by Dickinson Press.

We hope you enjoy this book from Northfield Publishing. Our goal is to provide high-quality, thought-provoking books and products that connect truth to your real needs and challenges. For more information on other books and products written and produced from a biblical perspective, go to www.moodypublishers.com or write to:

Northfield Publishing
215 West Locust Street
Chicago, IL 60610

3 5 7 9 10 8 6 4

To the many singles who during the past
thirty years have shared with me
their relationship struggles and joys.
May this book bring more joy and less struggle.

CONTENTS

ACKNOWLEDGMENTS

MANY STRANDS of influence have intertwined to produce this book. First, I was greatly influenced by those singles who read my original *Five Love Languages* book for married couples and encouraged me to write a sequel for singles. Without their encouragement I would never have begun the journey.

The second strand of influence was the scores of singles who shared with me their encounters with love, or the lack of love, which shaped their lives. Their stories keep this book from being an academic treatise. I have wept and danced with them, and I hope the reader will experience both the pain and the excitement of love. All names have been changed to protect the privacy of individuals, but their stories are true.

The words and paragraphs were keyboarded by Tricia Kube and Martha Jones. Tricia has been my administrative assistant for more than twenty years, and Martha has been my valuable part-time assistant. Kay Tatum was the computer guru who pulled all the technical strands to-gether and wove the individual chapters into a manuscript. Without the help of these three dedicated ladies, the words of this book would still be rolling around in my head.

Shannon Warden has served as my research assistant. She spent numerous hours interviewing singles and helping me weave their stories into the fabric of the five love language mosaic. She also produced the "love language profile" found in the conclusion of the book. I deeply appreciate her contribution.

The Moody Publishers team has done their usual job of encouraging me in the project. Randall Payleitner and Jim Vincent assisted me greatly in their editorial suggestions. Greg Thornton and Bill Thrasher believed in the project from the beginning and encouraged me to take the five love languages message to singles. The entire publishing team is committed to helping singles have loving relationships. Their personal interest in the book has motivated me to keep "weaving" the strands.

As always, my wife, Karolyn, has been supportive of this project. She has worked with me through the years as we have sought to develop friendships with singles. Our lives have been greatly enriched from these relationships. It is our hope that this book will encourage singles to pursue "love" above all else, knowing that to pursue love is to pursue God.

INTRODUCTION

MORE THAN FIFTEEN years ago I wrote *The Five Love Languages: How to Express Heartfelt Commitment to Your Mate.* The response has been far more than I ever anticipated: Total sales are now nearly five million copies. Each year the book has sold more copies than the year before. *The Five Love Languages* has been translated into forty-two languages around the world.

I have been asked on many occasions to explain its phenomenal success. The only answer I have is that its message focuses on our deepest emotional need: the need to feel loved. For married couples, it provides the insights and practical tools for keeping emotional love alive in a marriage. Thousands of couples have indicated that the idea of the five love languages brought "new life" to their marriage.

Because the book was written specifically to married couples, I did not anticipate that numerous single adults would also read it. I often encounter single adults like Jill, who said, "I know you wrote *The Five Love Languages* for married couples, but I want you to know that it has greatly helped me in all of my relationships." I meet singles like Robert, a senior in college, who told me, "I never understood my roommate until I read your book. You've got to write a version of *The Five Love Languages* for single adults." And so, my motivation for writing this edition comes from the many, many single adults who have expressed these same needs and desires.

Though my writing and counseling have focused primarily on marriage and family, I continually find myself right in the middle of a culture alive with single adults. Quite a few years ago, I started a single-adult ministry in the church that I attend and where I have served as a counselor for over thirty years. For nine years I immersed myself in the joys and struggles of single adults. We did all kinds of fun stuff together, living life alongside one another. Some of the small groups were focused more on "growth" for people who were doing well and we had "support" groups for those who were going through more difficult times. It was during these times of growth and support that I was able to spend hundreds of hours in individual counseling with single adults who faced an array of emotional and relational issues. That ministry is still a thriving part of our church family today.

Married or single, young or old, every human has the emotional need to feel loved. When this need is met, we move out to reach our potential for God and our potential for good in the world. However, when we feel unloved, we struggle just to survive. I am deeply convinced that the truths in this book will enable single adults to learn the skills that lead to loving and being loved.

Now it is important for you to understand that this volume is not a rehash of the original *Five Love Languages* with a new cover on it. The five love languages have not changed, of course, but in the following pages we will focus on their application to single adults. I am indebted to the hundreds of single adults who have shared their stories of how the five love languages have enhanced each of their relationships.

Nothing has more potential for enhancing one's sense of well-being than effectively loving and being loved. Whether you've never been married, you're divorced, or you're widowed, your deepest emotional need is to feel loved, and your greatest successes will be obtained by loving others. This book is designed to help you do both of these things effectively.

In the first two chapters, we will explore who single adults are and why love is the key to relationships. In chapters 3–7, you will learn about each of the five love languages. In chapter 8, you will discover your own primary love language and how to discover the love languages of others.

The remaining chapters will help you learn how to love and be loved by speaking these love languages. In chapter 9 you will discover how to apply the principles of the five love languages in understanding your parents, siblings, and the rest of your family. Chapters 10–11 will explore dating relationships, the possibility of marriage, and the importance of love languages in building a successful marriage relationship. Chapter 12 will focus on communicating love to roommates, classmates, and coworkers—the love languages aren't just for romantic relationships. Chapter 13 has guidelines for single parents communicating love to their children. Finally, in chapter 14, we'll focus on love as the key to success.

Come with me on this journey into the personal lives of dozens of singles adults who have found that life's greatest discovery is in learning how to give and receive love properly.

1

single adults:

SIGNIFICANT AND GROWING

IF YOU'RE READING this book, chances are you're either single or know someone who is. More than four of every ten American adults are single—92 million Americans.[1] In fact, the United States has more single adults than any other nation in the world except China and India.[2]

Of course, it wouldn't be accurate to lump all single adults into the same group. There are at least five very different categories of single adults. The largest numbers of singles are those who have never been down the aisle (those to whom this book is largely directed), but the other four groups also command our attention. Here are the five groups:

1. Never married. Age eighteen and older, this group is 49 million strong.[3] The median age of a first marriage has risen to twenty-five among women and twenty-seven among men. This means that, in the general population among people eighteen to twenty-four, almost four out of every five (78 percent) have never been married.[4]

2. Divorced. Today, at any one time, 10 percent of all adults are divorced.[5] Over time, however, many more married adults suffer through a divorce. Within five years of the wedding, 20 percent of all marriages end in divorce. Within ten years, one-third of all couples will be divorced, and within fifteen years, 43 percent will be divorced.[6]

3. *Separated but not divorced.* These are individuals who are still legally married but no longer live under the same roof. In lifestyle they are more single than married. The separated status, however, is temporary. These individuals will either reconcile with their spouses or go on and formalize their separation by legal divorce. Research indicates that 97 percent of white women (and 75 percent of non-white women) who separate from their husbands end up divorced within five years of the separation.[7]

4. *Widowed.* Widowhood is definitely gender biased. Four out of five adults who are single because of the death of their spouse are females. Nearly half of all women sixty-five and older are widowed, compared to only 14 percent of men over sixty-five.[8]

5. *Single parents.* One hundred years ago, fewer than 1 percent of adults was a single parent of a child under eighteen. Today there are more than twelve million single parents with children under eighteen in their care — almost one out of every three families.[9] Obviously, many single parents are also divorced. But a growing number of single parents have never been married. Among those who are single moms, 40 percent were never married to the father of their children.[10] Thus a growing number of never-married singles are also single parents.

DIVERSE YET UNITED

Clearly, single adults are a very diverse group of people. However, they are still united by those factors that hold all of us together as humans. Everyone wrestles with values, morals, relationships, and meaning. If you are a single adult, just like everyone else, you're seeking to understand yourself and your place in the world. At the heart of these pursuits is the need as an unmarried person to give and receive emotional love.

No matter which category you may or may not fall into, as a single adult, you want to feel loved by the significant people in your life. You also want to believe that others need your love. Giving and receiving love is at the center of every single adult's sense of well-being. If you feel loved and needed, you can survive the pressures of life. But without love, life can become exceedingly bleak.

THE MAN WITH THE METAL HALO

I first met Rob on one of my trips to the Grand Canyon (one of nature's most beautiful portraits). On the south rim of the canyon, somewhere near the Bright Angel Trail, I spotted Rob and two older adults. He wasn't hard to spot, because he was wearing a back brace with a metal halo that circled his head. I gave him a friendly nod and a smile, my way of saying hello.

Rob responded, "Hello, I hope you're having a good morning." His inviting smile beckoned me into conversation. I discovered that he had suffered spinal injuries in a hiking accident. The older couple were his mom and dad.

The three had planned a family trip to the Grand Canyon two years earlier. The first year money was a problem, so they postponed their dream. Then Rob had his accident and they couldn't leave home. Now that Rob was doing somewhat better, they had come to see the canyon. When the family originally planned the trip, they intended to hike to the foot of the canyon. Their dream had been altered but not destroyed. So they planned to spend the week enjoying the sights of the canyon.

Rob wheeled his chair into position for a great view of the trail and canyon, and he and his parents were soaking in the fabulous view. I com-

THE FIVE LOVE LANGUAGES — SINGLES EDITION

mended them for not giving up on their dream and wished them well.

My son and I continued our week together exploring the canyon. Toward the end of the week I ran into Rob in the lobby of the Bright Angel Lodge. Because of our earlier encounter, it seemed I was seeing an old friend. We ended up talking for two hours. Rob shared his story about the fall that resulted in his injuries and the determined efforts of the rescue workers who flew him out by helicopter. He told me about the pain and the emotional struggle of those early days when he wasn't sure he would ever be able to walk again. He had a number of brushes with depression, had lost a new job opportunity, and spent many weeks in physical therapy.

When I asked what had enabled him to come through that experience and still have such a vibrant spirit, his answer was simple. "Love," he said. "That's the only way I could have made it. Mom and Dad were with me through the whole thing, and I had a girlfriend . . . not a romantic relationship, but a close friend who came to see me every day in those early weeks. I don't think I would have made it without her. She brought me hope. She encouraged me in my therapy, and she prayed with me. I had never had a girl pray with me before. There was something about the way she talked to God that gave me hope. Her words were like rain on my parched emotions.

"We're still good friends. Her love and the love of my folks brought me through."

Then Rob added, "I hope someday I can help someone else the way they have helped me."

THE POWER OF LOVE

Rob is a living example — both of the power of love and the single adult's deep need to love and be loved. Love is the fundamental building block of all human relationships. It will greatly impact our values and morals. I am also convinced that love is the most important ingredient in the single's search for meaning.

That is why I feel compelled to write this book on the five love languages. What you will read in the following pages has the potential to enhance every area of your life. Reading this book will require time, but I assure you that it will be time well invested. You have likely invested time in learning the language of technology, right? Things like text messaging, searching the Internet, and social networking through Facebook. If so, you have reaped the benefits. Unfortunately, most single adults (and most people in general) know more about these things than they do about love. The reason for this is obvious: they have spent more time perfecting technology and less time studying love.

SOMETHING'S MISSING

I agree with Professor Leo Buscaglia, who said:

> *Psychologists, psychiatrists, sociologists, anthropologists and educators have suggested in countless studies and numerous research papers that love is a "learned response, a learned emotion." . . . Most of us continue to behave as though love is not learned but lies dormant in each human being and simply awaits some mystical age of awareness to emerge in full bloom. Many wait for this age forever. We seem to refuse to face the obvious fact that most of us spend our lives trying to find love, trying to live in it and dying without ever truly discovering it.*[11]

I have invested the past thirty plus years of my life in helping people discover how to emotionally connect with each other—how to actively give and receive love, not passively wait for it to somehow magically happen. I can say with confidence to all singles—whether never married, once married, or married several times—that if you will read and apply the information given in the following chapters, you will discover how to give and receive love more effectively. You will discover the missing ingredient in some of your past relationships, and you will learn how to build wholesome, supportive relationships by learning to speak other people's primary love language and better understand your own primary love language.

Much of the pain in broken relationships in our world stems from the truth that many of us in Western culture have never been serious students of love. We haven't really taken it seriously enough to learn how it actually works. In the following pages you will meet dozens of single adults from all categories and all ages who have discovered that a proper understanding of love really does have the potential to change the world—and, more succinctly, to change individual relationships.

THINGS TO THINK ABOUT

1. To what degree do you feel loved by the significant people in your life?

2. In a time of need, have you experienced the love of a friend like the one Rob described: "I don't think I would have made it without her"? If so, how did your friend show his or her love?

3. Have you been a friend to someone in need? How did you express your love?

4. How successful have you been in giving and receiving emotional love?

5. How interested are you in studying the nature of love and learning new ways to express love?

2

this is it:

THE KEY TO YOUR RELATIONSHIPS

WE ARE RELATIONAL creatures. All humans live in community, and most people seek social interaction. In Western culture, isolation is seen as one of the most stringent of punishments. Even hardened criminals do not generally aspire to solitary confinement.

It is safe to assume that everyone reading this book has relationships. The question is: What is the quality of these relationships?

Positive and affirming relationships bring great pleasure, but poor relationships can bring deep pain. I would be so bold as to suggest that life's greatest happiness is found in good relationships, and life's deepest hurt is found in bad relationships. If you feel loved by your mother, then the maternal relationship brings you a feeling of comfort and encouragement. On the other hand, if your relationship with your mother is fractured, you probably suffer feelings of abandonment. And if you were abused by your mother, you likely feel hurt and anger, maybe even hatred.

OUR PARENTS

Lack of love from parents often motivates children to go searching for love in other relationships. This search is often misguided and leads to further disappointment. For a number of years my son, Derek, has worked with "street" people. A few years ago he said to me, "I've never met anyone on the street who had a good relationship with his or her father."

Whether you want them to or not, all of your relationships spring from the relationship you have with your parents. The nature of that relationship will have a positive—or negative—influence on all other relationships.

Many single adults have felt unloved by one or both parents. To compensate for the emptiness, they have poured themselves into positive pursuits and have accomplished admirable goals in many areas, but they have been extremely unsuccessful in building positive relationships with other adults. Most have never stopped to ask, "What do I need to learn about love in order to build successful, positive relationships?" Understanding the five love languages will answer that question.

THE STAGES OF A ROMANTIC RELATIONSHIP

Relationships are never static. All of us experience changes in relationships, but few of us stop to analyze why a relationship gets better or worse. Most divorced singles did not enter marriage with a goal of divorcing. In fact, most of them were extremely happy when they married. They would have characterized their marital relationship as positive, loving, and affirming. Obviously something happened to the relationship. By the time they divorce they are saying such things as, "My spouse is unloving, uncaring, self-centered, and sometimes downright mean." Ironically, the other spouse often makes similar statements about them. What happened?

With thousands of marriages ending in divorce every year, isn't it time to stop and ask why? Why do good marriages go bad? Why do people become single again? After thirty years as a marriage counselor, I am convinced that the answer lies in the misunderstanding that most people have about the nature of love.

Western society is largely addicted to romantic love. If you doubt that, listen to our songs, watch our movies, and check the sales statistics on romance novels. On the other hand, we're very ignorant of the facts about love. We have bought into the concept that love is something that happens to you. It is magical, obsessive, and extremely exhilarating. If you have it, you have it; and if you don't, you don't, and there is nothing you can do about it. While this description of love can be fairly accurate, it only describes the first stage of a romantic relationship. It certainly does not describe the second and more important stage of romantic love. Let's look at these two stages of a relationship.

Stage One: The Obsessive Stage of Love

Did you know there has been extensive scientific research done on the "in love," obsessive stage of love? The late Prof. Dorothy Tennov wrote a classic book, *Love and Limerence*, in which she concluded that the average lifespan of this stage of love is two years.[1] During this obsessive stage of love, we live under the illusion that the person with whom we are in love is perfect…at least, perfect for us. Our friends can see his or her flaws, but we cannot. Your mother may say, "Honey, have you considered that he hasn't had a steady job in five years?" Your response may be, "Mom, give him a break. He's waiting for the right opportunity." Your coworker may say, "Have you considered that she's been married four times before?" to which you respond, "Those guys were all losers before. The woman deserves to be happy. I'm going to make her happy."

During this initial stage of love, we have other irrational thoughts, such as, "I'll never be happy unless we are together forever. Nothing else in life really matters." Such thinking often leads a student to drop out of college and marry his or her lover, or to start living together even though they are not married. In this stage of love, differences are minimized or denied. We just know that we are happy, that we have never been happier, and we intend to be this happy for the rest of our lives.

This stage of love does not require a lot of effort. I was in the Philadelphia International Airport one afternoon when a young lady I'll call Carrie walked up to me and introduced herself. She reminded me that we had met at a conference some two years earlier. During our conversation I learned she would be getting married in about six weeks. In fact, she was on her way to see her fiancé, who was stationed at a naval base near Chicago. When I told her I was on my way to lead a marriage seminar, she asked, "What do you teach at those?"

"I help couples learn how to work on their marriage."

"I don't understand," Carrie replied. "Why would you have to work on a marriage? If you have to work on it, doesn't that mean you probably shouldn't have gotten married in the first place?"

She was voicing a commonly believed myth about love. The myth contains some truth, but it is only a partial truth. What is true is that love requires little work during its initial stage. One doesn't work to fall in love. It just happens.

It all begins with what I call the "tingles." There's something about the way the other person looks, the way he (or she) talks, the way he emotes, the way he carries himself that gives you a little tingle inside. It is the tingles that motivate us to ask someone out for a cup of coffee. Sometimes we lose the tingles on the first date. Something they do or say annoys us, or we find out they have a habit that we know we can't tolerate.

Therefore, the next time they call for a cup of coffee, we're not really that thirsty. It's fine with us if we never see the person again, and the tingles die a quick, natural death.

But with others, every time we go out for a cup of coffee, we can hardly wait to meet for the next cup of coffee, we love coffee so much! The tingles get stronger and stronger, and the emotional obsession begins to set in. We find ourselves thinking about the person as soon as we wake up. He or she is the last person we think of before we go to sleep. All day long, we're wondering what the person is doing. We can hardly wait to be together again, and every time we're together, it's so perfect.

Eventually one of us says to the other something like, "I think I could love you." We are testing the waters to see if they are feeling what we are feeling. And if they give us a positive response, such as "What would be so bad about that?" we will gaze longingly into each other's eyes deep into the night. The next time the moon is right, we actually say the words "I love you." And we wait until they respond, "I love you too." From that moment, the emotional obsession grows until we are certain that we want to spend the rest of our lives together.

It is in this obsessed stage of love that most people get married, and others start living together. The whole relationship has been effortless. We have been swept along by the heightened emotions of the "in love" obsession. That's why my friend in the airport could not comprehend working on a marriage. She anticipated that their marriage would continue in this euphoric state in which each of them freely gave to the other, and each viewed the other as the most important person in the universe.

Wait . . . There's a second stage of love?

While Carrie understood stage one of love, she had no comprehension of stage two. She was not even aware that there was a stage two.

Her perceptions of love are typical for both single and married adults in Western culture. That is why understanding the five love languages is so critical if we are to have long-term relationships. The five love languages reveal how to keep emotional love alive once we come down from the emotional high of the obsessive stage of love.

Without this knowledge, four out of five individuals who divorce will remarry and repeat the cycle with another mate. Sixty percent of those who remarry will experience a second divorce and be single again…unless they learn the true nature of love and move successfully from stage one to stage two.

Stage Two: The Covenant Stage of Love

Stage two is what I prefer to call "covenant" love. It is very different from stage one, which I sometimes call "passionate" or "obsessive" love. I do not mean to imply that covenant love is not passionate, but in covenant love, passion must be fed and nurtured. It will not continue to flow simply because we remain in the relationship. It is truly different from stage one. The obsessiveness we have had for each other begins to fade, and we recognize that there are other important pursuits in life in addition to pursuing each other. The illusions of perfection evaporate, and the words of your mother return to your mind: "He hasn't had a steady job in five years" . . . or you remember the words of your coworker: "The woman has been married four times before." And now, in your mind, you begin to agree with your mother (or your coworker). You wonder how you could have been so blind to these realities.

The differences in personality, interests, and lifestyles become very obvious, when before, you hardly saw them. The euphoria that led you to put each other first and to focus on each other's well-being has now dissipated, and you begin to focus on yourself and realize that your lover is no longer meeting your needs. So you begin to request and then demand of the person, and when he or she refuses to meet your demands, you withdraw or you lash out in anger. Your anger or withdrawal pushes your lover further away and makes it more difficult for him/her to express love to you.

Can such a tarnished relationship be reborn? The answer is yes. But only if the couple comes to understand the nature of love and learns how to express love in a language the other person can receive.

The obsessive stage is over. The couple may be dating or married, but they must move to the next stage, or the romantic relationship will end.

Covenant love is conscious love. It is intentional love. It is a commitment to love no matter what. It requires thought and action. It does not wait for the encouragement of warm emotions but chooses to look out for the interest of the other because you are committed to their well-being.

Our behavior will affect our partner's emotions. In fact, if we learn to express love in the other person's love language, he/she will feel loved. And if that person reciprocates by speaking our love language, he/she will meet our emotional need for love. And we will have made the transition from the euphoria of passionate love to the deep, settled confidence of covenant love. We love each other, and our love will endure because we *choose* to nurture love by learning how to express love effectively.

It is covenant love that sustains a relationship through the years and leads the fifty-year-old husband to say about his wife, "I love her more deeply now than the day we married."

Covenant love requires two factors: knowledge of the nature of love and the will to love. Understanding the five love languages will give you the information you need to have a successful long-term covenant love relationship. Hopefully, as you see the benefits of covenant love, you will also find the will to love.

So, here is the thesis of this book based on thirty-plus years of experience in the counseling office: I am convinced there are only five fundamental love languages — five ways to express love emotionally. In the following chapters we will discuss each of the five. Of the five love languages, each of us has a primary language. One of the five speaks more deeply to us emotionally than the other four. We can receive love through all five, but if we don't receive our primary love language, we will not feel loved even though the person is speaking the other four. However, if they speak our primary love language sufficiently, then the other four provide icing on the cake.

THE RIGHT LANGUAGE

The problem is that, by nature, we tend to speak our own love language. That is, we express love to others in a language that would make us feel loved. But if it is not his or her primary love language, it will not mean to them what it would mean to us.

This is why thousands of couples are frustrated. Sam, a divorced single, said about the woman he is dating: "I don't understand her. She says she feels like I don't love her. How could she feel unloved? Every day I tell her that I love her. I also give her compliments every day. I tell her how pretty she is. I tell her what a good mother she is. How could she feel unloved?"

The problem is that her love language is acts of service, not words of affirmation. She's thinking: *If he loved me he would do something to help me. When he comes over, he watches television while I wash the dishes. He never helps me with anything. I'm sick of his words "I love you. I love you." Words are cheap. If he really loved me, he would do something. I do everything for him; he does nothing for me.* This scenario is repeated in thousands of relationships. Each person speaks his own language and does not understand why the other does not feel loved. If we want the other person to feel loved, we must discover and learn to speak his/her primary love language.

Many dating relationships become troubled, especially if the couple dates beyond the two-year obsessive stage of passionate love. Often these couples break up and go their separate ways, not because they would not have made good marital partners, but because they lost the emotional love they had for each other. Often this could have been remedied had they discovered each other's primary love language and learned to speak it.

FIVE LANGUAGES FOR ALL TYPES OF RELATIONSHIPS

So far in this chapter I have discussed the male-female relationship and focused on the dating side of things; however, the five love languages apply in all human relationships. Some single adults do not feel loved by their parents, not because their parents did not love them, but because their parents never learned to speak their primary love language. Many single adults have been unsuccessful in their vocational ambitions, not because they lack skills to perform their job, but because they have never learned how to express appreciation to those who work with them and for them. Consequently, relationships become strained and productivity is hampered, often leading them to seek another job or being asked to seek another job. Still others are frustrated by long-term friendships in which they or their friends feel unloved or unappreciated and struggle to better understand each other.

Learning to speak love and appreciation in a language the other person can receive is the key to enhancing all human relationships. I can assure you that if you read the following chapters and apply the principles of the five love languages, you will become more effective in all of your relationships. The principles in the rest of this book are the same truths

I have shared with hundreds of people in my counseling office. I have every reason to believe the principles will be as effective for you as they have been for them.

The next five chapters will provide an in-depth look at each of the five love languages. Read through each one with both yourself and the people in your life in mind.

THINGS TO THINK ABOUT

1. Which of your relationships do you consider to be healthy?

2. Which of your relationships would you like to see improved?

3. How would you describe your relationship with your mother? Your father?

4. In dating relationships, how many times have you experienced Stage One: Passionate Love?

5. Were you able to make the transition to Stage Two: Covenant Love? Why or why not?

6. Are you willing to invest time in learning to speak the five love languages?

3

love language #1:

WORDS OF AFFIRMATION

PSYCHOLINGUISTICS is the study of the effect of language on personality. We have all been greatly influenced by the words we've heard through the years. Some single adults grew up in a positive linguistic environment. They heard words that emphasized the pleasant, joyful, and beautiful aspects of life. Others grew up in a more negative linguistic environment. Children who grow up in these contrasting environments will hear totally different vocabularies resulting in vastly different personalities and behavior patterns. The ancient Hebrew proverb did not overstate the impact of words: "The tongue has the power of life and death."[1]

Since words hold such influential power, it is understandable that words of affirmation would be one of the five fundamental languages of love. Single adults who grew up in a negative linguistic environment will probably have greater difficulty learning to speak words of affirmation. For some, it will mean learning a whole new vocabulary while seeking to delete the negative words that so freely flow from their mouths. It will also involve learning to listen, really listen, to the affirming words of others.

Let me make this clear from the outset: My desire as you read this book is that you will learn both to receive and give love in all five love languages. I am assuming that those who take time to read a book on love desire to become better persons, to have better relationships, and to reach their potential of leaving a positive impact on the world. It is my sincere belief that learning to speak and understand the five love languages will help you reach these objectives.

The good news is that all of these languages can be learned. In this chapter, we are focusing on learning to give and receive words of affirmation. For some people this is their primary love language, but all of us need to be able to speak it. And no matter if it is our primary language or not we all enjoy hearing it. So, how can we best develop this language?

For some singles, this is already their native tongue. They grew up in a positive linguistic environment, hearing many affirming words from their earliest childhood. It will be relatively easy for them to speak this language, because they have been practicing it for many years. These are the people who are known in their social circle as encouragers. They are constantly affirming, encouraging, and expressing words of appreciation to others.

For others, words of affirmation will be a foreign language. They have never learned to receive or speak such words. Throughout this chapter I will give practical ideas on how to learn to speak this love language. Let me begin to describe the nature of this language, and the potential influence it holds on human relationships, by introducing you to Brian.

I met Brian at a singles conference a few years ago. He was a tall, handsome young man. He was the kind of guy the girls noticed and talked about with their friends later at night. However, I discovered that Brian had not been very successful with girls in the past. In fact, that's why he requested to talk to me.

BRIAN: FOOTBALL HERO AND RELATIONSHIP FAILURE

He had played football in both high school and college and had enough going for him that it could all have easily gone to his head, but none of that seemed very important to Brian. "What does it take to play football?" he asked. Then he proceeded to answer his own question. "A strong body, a brain, and a lot of hard work. But what bothers me is 'relationships.' This is much more difficult than anything I ever experienced playing football."

Then, with a rather forlorn look, he said, "I'm getting older. I'm doing well in my career. But I want to get married. I want to have a family. But at this point, I don't even have a girlfriend. I can't seem to get close to anyone. I've dated, but it never goes anywhere."

I could tell that Brian was perplexed and serious. I began by asking, "What's the longest time you've ever dated one girl?"

"About four months," he responded. "Actually, I dated one girl for about three months and another girl for about four months. The rest of them have been for shorter times."

"Do the girls typically end the relationship, or are you the one who breaks it off?" I asked.

"Usually the girls," he said. "Once or twice I've dated people that I wasn't really interested in, so I didn't ask them out again."

"Did any of the girls ever tell you why she didn't want to date you any longer?"

"Well, the one I dated three months said that she didn't think we had a lot in common, and the other girl said that she just didn't think we were compatible, whatever that means." Then he added, "I don't know. I think it has something to do with the fact that I'm not a very good conversationalist."

"When It Gets Personal . . ."

"I don't mean that I can't talk. Actually, I do a lot of talking. But it's about my job or my family or her job and her family. It's like I don't know how to talk about us. When it gets personal, I don't know what to say."

I sensed that Brian was on the right trail, so I said to him, "When you were growing up, what kind of relationship did you have with your father?"

He thought a moment and said, "Strained. My father had an alcohol problem. He seldom came to any of my games in high school or college. When he did, he was very critical of the way I played. I'll never forget what he said the one time he came to see me play college football. He said, 'You'll never make it to the pros playing like that.'

"I remember how devastated I was. I went out and got drunk that night and tried not to think about what my father had said, but I've never been able to get away from those words. That's probably why I never gave serious thought again to playing pro football."

"When you were younger, was your father also critical?" I asked.

"Yeah, especially when he was drinking," Brian said. "Nothing was ever right when he was drinking. He criticized me and Mom."

"And what about your mother?" I inquired. "What kind of relationship did you have with her?"

"Mom was depressed a lot," he said. "She had a hard life. She fixed my meals and washed my clothes and those kinds of things. But we didn't have a very close relationship, especially when I got to be a teenager. She was pretty much on my case about homework and getting home on time. I remember in high school she was always saying I shouldn't let football interfere with my studies."

A Home of Discouraging Words

Clearly Brian grew up in a negative linguistic environment. Most of the things he heard from his parents were critical or discouraging words. So I said to him, "When you were dating Courtney and Amy, what did you find attractive about them?" He seemed rather shocked at my question, but he stumbled to answer.

"Uh, well, they were both good-looking," he said. "Courtney was a lot of fun; Amy was quieter, but very sincere. One of the things that I liked about her was her spiritual commitment. She was a strong Christian, and I liked that. I also liked her family; her mom and dad had a good marriage, and they seemed to like me. Courtney liked to go to movies and ride bikes. I had never been into biking, but it was pretty exciting. We went on a couple of all-day trips. Both girls were college graduates and smart. I liked that about both of them."

"Do you ever remember complimenting either of the girls about the way they were dressed?" There was a long pause, and then Brian said, "I don't know. They both just dressed normal. I don't remember much about the way they dressed. It was always fine."

"So you don't remember ever saying to one of them, 'You look nice today'?"

"No, I don't think so."

"Do you ever remember making a statement similar to this to Courtney: 'You made a really great choice on that movie. I really enjoyed it'?"

"I liked most of her movies. I only got upset once or twice when I didn't like the story line."

I wasn't sure Brian heard my question, so I repeated, "Did you ever tell her that you appreciated the movie she picked out?" His response was very revealing.

"I think she knew that I liked the movies," he said.

It was obvious to me but not obvious to Brian that he had never learned to speak the love language known as words of affirmation.

I wasn't certain that I could communicate to Brian in one conversation what I was seeing, but I made an attempt: "Brian, I hope that I can share with you what I am sensing, because I think it will help you in future relationships. You grew up in a home environment where you did not receive many words of affirmation. In fact, what you received primarily were critical, condemning words. You still remember some of those words, even as an adult, because they hurt so deeply. It doesn't mean that your parents were bad people or that they didn't love you. But it does mean that you didn't always feel their love."

I noticed that Brian's eyes were getting moist, and I knew that he was emotionally hearing what I was saying. However, I was not ready for his next statement. The tears were flowing freely now, and he said, "I guess every man would like to hear his father say that he is proud of him. I never heard that and I never felt that from my father. In fact, I don't ever remember hearing my father say the words 'I love you' or 'I'm proud of you.' But I'm grown now. I shouldn't let that affect me. I can't do anything about it. So why am I crying?"

Brian was smiling now, wiping the tears from his face, feeling a little ashamed.

I responded, "You're crying because what we are talking about is very important. All of us want to feel loved and appreciated by our parents. One of the ways we feel love is by hearing words of affirmation. That's what you wanted to hear from your parents. That's what all of us want to hear. But what you heard instead were critical words. These words brought hurt rather than help. I think there is something that can be done to correct the past. But first I want to focus on your relationship with girls, and what I'm about to say may cause you to cry even more than you've been crying. I think one of the reasons you have had difficulty in relationships is that, because you never heard the love language called words of affirmation, you don't know how to speak it to others.

"You said to me that you don't remember ever saying to either Courtney or Amy, 'You look nice in that dress or that outfit.' You don't remember saying to Courtney, 'You made a good choice in that movie. I really liked it.' In fact, you've said that when it came to personal things, you didn't know how to 'talk about us,' which leads me to believe that you have wonderful skills of talking about other things such as football, vocation, family, politics, weather, and sports, but you have never learned how to give affirming words on a personal level.

"Girls are people who like to be affirmed verbally, just as men like to be affirmed verbally. They tend to pull away from dating partners who do not give affirmation. Lack of verbal affirmation is interpreted as lack of love."

Brian's Discovery

Brian was no longer crying, but he shook his head back and forth as he spoke: "How could I have missed this? You're right; I don't affirm people.

"In fact, I'm often critical. I remember getting upset with Courtney about being late to a date once, and I talked to her about not being responsible. In fact, there were several times with both Amy and Courtney that I pointed out areas where I thought they needed growth. I realize now I was criticizing them just like my father criticized me. Why didn't I see this?" Once more Brian was crying.

I knew this could be a major turning point in Brian's life, so I sat quietly as he cried and put my hand on his shoulder. After a few minutes he asked, "Is there any hope? How can I give what I never received?"

I'm sure that Brian never anticipated our conversation would take us to such depths, but we were there now, and there was no turning back. So I said, "Brian, there is hope. That's the marvelous thing about being human. We can change our future. We need not be enslaved by experiences of the past. We can learn to love even when we have not received love." In fact, learning to love others is the fastest way to receive love.

TIME FOR ACTION

Brian's Christian faith was important to him, so I reminded him of the words of Jesus. "Give, and it will be given to you."[2] I also reminded him that the Scriptures say, "We love Him because He first loved us."[3] "The same principle is true in human relationships," I said. "If we want to be loved, and all of us do, then the first step is to express love to others."

"Can you help me?" Brian asked.

"I can and I will," I said, "but not right now. I have an appointment in five minutes. But if you will meet me at nine o'clock tonight in the lobby, and bring a notebook, I will give you some ideas on how you can learn to speak the love language of words of affirmation."

"I'll be here," he said.

I gave Brian a hug and walked away, knowing that this could be one of the most important days in his life.

Opening the Notebook

When I arrived at nine o'clock that evening, Brian was sitting there ready to go with his notebook. "I really appreciate you taking time to meet with me," he said. "I know you must be tired by now."

"Tired, but hopefully still awake," I said.

"I've been thinking about our conversation all afternoon," Brian said. "It all makes so much sense. I don't know how I missed it all these years."

"Well, what's important now is that we do something about it," I suggested. "Are you ready?"

"I'm ready," he said while opening his notebook.

We began by talking about his mom and dad. His dad had been sober for the last several years, but once in a while he "falls off the wagon," Brian said. Because of a new job, Brian saw his parents about once every three months.

"How often do you talk with them on the telephone or e-mail them?" I asked.

"Well, neither one of them really does e-mail, but I do call about once a week just to make sure they are doing all right."

"Okay," I said. "The first principle is: *Start where you are.*" Brian wrote it in his notebook, "Start where you are." I could tell he was ready to learn.

"Let me describe where I think you are. This is a summary of what we talked about this morning. You are now an adult, an adult who never remembers ever hearing his father say the words 'I love you. I'm proud of you, Son,' and an adult who has few memories of his mother making positive comments. Is that correct?"

Brian nodded yes.

"Through the years you have tried to push the hurt out of your heart and tell yourself that it didn't matter, but it's obvious from our conversation this morning that it does matter.

"The second principle is: *Be active, not passive.*" Brian was writing again.

"Until now your approach has been passive. You've suffered in silence. Starting today I want to encourage you to take action. The choice to love is the choice to take initiative. It is the choice to do or say something for the other person's benefit, something that would help make them a better person, something that would enrich their lives or make life more meaningful for them.

Affirming Your Parents

"One way to express love is by giving words of affirmation, which brings us to the third principle: *Choose a strategy for loving or expressing love.* Here's the strategy I want to suggest. The next time you call home, when you end the conversation with your mom or your dad, end it by saying, 'I love you, Mom' or 'I love you, Dad.' Okay? Their response doesn't matter. The important thing is that you are taking the initiative to express words of affirmation to them, and your strategy is using the telephone to do this.

"After you do this the first time, it will be easier to repeat it the second time and the third. For the next three months I want to encourage you to end every phone conversation to your folks with the words 'I love you.' At the end of three months I want you to add another statement. After 'I love you, Dad,' I want you to add the words 'I appreciate what you have done for me through the years,' and use the statement with your mother. Use these statements for the second three months.

"Does this sound like something you could do?"

"I think so," Brian said. "I guess the first time will be the hardest."

"Now, let me make sure that we are on the same page. Are both of these statements true? 'I love you, Mom,' and 'I love you, Dad.' Remember, love is the attitude which wishes good things for the other person. Do you desire the best possible life for your mom and dad for the rest of their years?"

"Yes," Brian said.

"Then 'I love you' is a true statement."

"Yes."

"Is this statement true: 'I appreciate what you've done for me through the years'? I assume your mother did some good things for you."

"Yes," Brian said.

"And your father worked and paid the bills and other things?"

"Yes," Brian agreed.

"So, those statements are true — 'I love you,' and 'I appreciate what you've done for me through the years'?"

"Yes, they are," Brian said.

"Then what I'm asking is that you verbalize the truth to your parents. Words of affirmation are simply true statements affirming the worth of another person.

"If you will try this, I can almost guarantee you that before six months is over both of your parents will begin to give you affirming words as well. You are not doing it in order to get their affirmation; you're doing it because you choose to love them. But the fact is, love stimulates love, and you are choosing to take the initiative rather than to wait for them to take the initiative."

A Place to Start

"Okay," said Brian, "I can do this. But how is this going to help me in my dating relationships?"

"It's a first step," I said. "If you can learn to give love to your parents by affirming words, then you can learn to give them to the girls you date. But that's not the next step. Right now you don't have a girlfriend, right?"

"That's true," Brian said.

"So, I want you to apply this principle in your vocational relationships. You do interact with people in your job. Is that correct? Then I want you to set a goal of giving a verbal affirmation to someone with whom you work at least once a week for the next three months."

Making a List

I gave Brian a list of the kinds of things he could say. They included the following:

- "Thanks for taking that phone call. I really didn't have time to talk to him, and you handled it well."
- "You always have such a positive attitude. I appreciate that."
- "You did a great job with this. Thanks."
- "The boss told me what you did. Thanks for making me look good."
- "When you do things, you always do them right. I really appreciate that about you."

"Do you ever see the janitor where you work?" I asked Brian.

"Not often, but once in a while if I'm working late I'll see a janitor."

"Then how about saying, 'I appreciate your taking the trash out every night. We couldn't make it around here without you'?"

He wrote that in his notebook, along with the rest of the list. Brian came up with a couple more affirming statements. One made me chuckle. "I could thank the guy who makes the coffee every morning," he said.

"What would you say to him?" I asked.

"I could say, 'Dan, thanks for making the coffee every morning. Even though I don't drink it, I really love the smell.'"

"Great! In the coming weeks I want to encourage you to add to that list in your notebook and every week express a statement of appreciation to someone with whom you work."

Brian said, smiling, "Okay, but what about my dating relationships?"

"I can tell you're into this dating thing," I replied.

"I'm getting older, Dr. Chapman. I want to get married, and dating usually goes before marriage."

Brian was smiling, but I could tell he was sincere. "Okay," I said, "on another page of your notebook I want you to begin to write the kinds of statements that you might make to a girl you are dating, statements that would affirm her worth. You might even think of people you've dated in the past and ask yourself, 'What might I have said to them that would have been affirming?'

"Let's go back to what we talked about this morning, such statements as 'You look nice in that outfit' and 'You made an excellent choice of movies. I really enjoyed this one.'" Brian began writing again. "Now, what else might you have said to Courtney?"

There was a long pause, and then Brian said, "I might have said, 'Your eyes are beautiful.'"

"Were they?" I asked.

"Yes, they were. That's one of the things that attracted me to her. Her eyes sparkled."

"Then add that to your affirmation list: 'Your eyes are beautiful. They sparkle.'"

"Oh man, this is getting really personal. I don't know if I can do it."

"Well, I'm not suggesting the first date, Brian, but somewhere along the line dating gets personal."

"I know," he said, "and that's my problem."

"And you're learning how to overcome your problem. By the time you have another girlfriend, you will have had six months' experience with your parents and three months' experience with people at work. I can assure you that you will be able to say it when the time comes."

We went on building our list. It included the following:

- "I like the way you relate to your mother. You treat her with respect, but you don't let her control your life."
- "Thanks for letting me take you out tonight. I really enjoyed our time together."
- "Your endurance puts me to shame. I'm going to have to practice more before I ride bikes with you again."
- "I loved the apple pie. Thanks for all the work you put into it."

I wasn't sure what Brian would do with his notebook, but I knew that he had a plan for enhancing his relationships with women. I was pleased when I saw him a year later at another singles conference. With great excitement he introduced me to his girlfriend, Rachel. "We've been dating for five months," he said, "and Rachel is the best." Rachel smiled and I smiled.

BRIAN AND HIS PARENTS

His Mom

Later, in private conversation, Brian shared his experiences with his mom and dad. The first time he said the words "I love you" to his mother at the end of a phone conversation, his mother said, "I love you too."

"I couldn't believe my ears," Brian told me. "I thought it would be two months before she said anything positive. After that, every time I said, 'I love you,' she said, 'I love you too.' Things were going so well that I moved the schedule up and after two months said to her, 'I love you, and I really appreciate all the things you have done for me through the years,' to which she responded, 'Brian, I wish I had done a lot more for you. I was so depressed in your early years that I am afraid I didn't give you the attention you needed.'

"I didn't know what to say, so I said, 'Well, I appreciate what you did, Mom, and I love you.' And she said, 'I love you too.'

"After that I started thinking, what did Mom do for me and what do I appreciate? So I made me a list, and at the end of each phone conversation I would tell her one thing I remembered that she did for me and how much I appreciated it. Before the six months was over, Mom and I were having great conversations. She had asked me to forgive her for not being a better mom, and I assured her that she did a lot of things that I really appreciated."

His Dad

The story of his relationship with his father was somewhat different. The first time Brian said the words "I love you," his father responded, "What?" to which Brian replied, "I love you, Dad."

"Oh, okay," he said.

The second time Brian talked to his father was about three weeks later. He repeated the "I love you" at the end of his phone conversation, and his father said, "Yeah, okay . . ."

Brian talked to his mother more often than his father because she usually answered the phone. So it was about three months later when Brian's father finally said, "I love you too."

"It was like a wave of emotion came over me when I hung up the phone," Brian told me. "In my mind I knew my father loved me, but I had never heard him say the words. It was incredible.

"After that, every time I said, 'I love you,' Dad said, 'I love you too.' When I added the words 'I appreciate all you've done for me through the years,' my father said, 'Well, it wasn't enough.'

"'But I want you to know I appreciate what you did, Dad, and I love you.'"

"I love you too," his dad replied.

Brian explained how he began to tell his dad how he appreciated specific things he had done for him.

"After a while Dad was telling me that he regretted not attending more of my football games and being more involved in my life. He said he was learning about forgiveness at church and asked me if I would forgive him. My immediate response was, 'Sure, Dad, you know I'll forgive you.'"

One weekend when he was at his parents' home Brian said to his father, "Dad, I'm proud of the way you are going to church and learning things about God and life. I'm really proud of you for that."

"Son, I'm proud of you. I could not imagine having a better son than you."

Brian reached out and hugged his dad, who then embraced Brian.

"I don't know that there were tears in my Dad's eyes, but there were certainly tears in my eyes. Our relationship has been different since then.

"I appreciate the time you spent with me last year," Brian told me. "I had no idea it would make such a difference in my life. I'm taking it slow with Rachel, but I can assure you I'm giving her words of affirmation. Want to see my notebook?"

"Sure," I responded.

He opened it up and showed me four pages of affirming statements he had made to Rachel. Brian had learned to speak words of affirmation.

SPEAKING THE DIFFERENT DIALECTS OF AFFIRMING WORDS
Words of Encouragement

Affirming words is one of the five basic love languages. Within that language, however, there are many dialects. In my time with Brian we fo-

~ AFFIRM ~ENCOURAGE ~PRAISE~APPERCIATE~KIND WORDS

"You are..."

"Thanks for..."

"I appreciate..."

AH - welcome to our fellow I'm mad you joined our fellowhip

VL - you are great w/ crafts & always comes up w/ fun thing for fun

EY — you're the Man @ golf, keep it going

ML Thanks for letting us use your house for fellowhip   you're always have a positive
attitude/
happy

MD →

LK Thanks for helping w/ the dinner and being flexible

MK you are a good friend neat @ you're a great bball teammate

EC I appreciate your honesty

SL keep doing what you are doing w/ youth

JJ thanks for being our fellowhip leader

VM you are a great friend

cused primarily on *words of appreciation*: expressing sincere gratitude for some act of service rendered. But there are also *words of encouragement*. The word *encourage* means "to inspire courage." All of us have areas in which we feel insecure. We lack courage and that lack of courage often hinders us from accomplishing the positive things we would like to do.

The latent potential within a work colleague or your roommate may await your encouraging words. Maybe someone in your circle of friendships has expressed an interest in learning to be an actor or actress. If it appears to you that they have potential (and almost all of us do), why not encourage them to explore their desire? Tell them that you can "see them doing that." If they are inexperienced, encourage them to attend a class at a local college. If they have had some experience, encourage them to audition for the local "little theatre." Many noble pursuits await the encouragement of a friend.

A friend says to you, "I've got to lose weight." What is your response? Will you "brush it off" by saying, "All of us need to lose weight"? Will you discourage your friend by saying, "That's one of the hardest things in the world to do," or "Even if you lose weight you'll probably put it back on again"? Or will you give the person encouraging words, such as "If you decide to do it, I know you will succeed because you are the kind of person who accomplishes goals"?

Words of Praise

Then there is the *dialect of praise*: recognizing someone's accomplishment. To a greater or lesser degree, all of us are achievers. We set goals to accomplish things. When we accomplish them, we like to be recognized. Hollywood has its Oscars. The world of music has its Grammy Awards, Dove Awards, and Country Music Awards. Athletic events have their trophies, and businesses distribute plaques. In personal relationships, words of praise meet the need for recognition.

Occasionally we all need someone to pat us on the shoulder and say, "Wow, that's great. I really like that. You did an excellent job." Think of what would happen in the world if all of us started praising each other for accomplishments rather than pointing out what was wrong.

The singles' world is filled with people who are worthy of praise. The single mom who works to support her family and to educate her children deserves the highest accolades. The person who works through the pain of divorce and comes out with a positive attitude believing in the future deserves praise. The single adult who wrestles with cancer and maintains a positive attitude by using his or her energies in positive pursuits is worthy of a whole praise team. The never-married single who invests time and energy in helping underprivileged children accomplish educational goals deserves words of praise. All around us there are people who daily expend energy for the benefit of others. These people need to hear words of praise.

Kind Words   & appreciation

Another dialect of words of affirmation is *kind words*. This has to do not only with what we say but the manner in which we say it. The same sentence can have two different meanings, depending on how you say it. The statement "I love you," when said with kindness and tenderness, can be a genuine expression of love. But what about the statement, "I, love you?" The question mark changes the whole meaning of those three words.

Sometimes our words are saying one thing, but our tone of voice is saying another. We are sending double messages. People usually interpret our message based on our tone of voice, not the words we use.

When your roommate says in a snarling tone, "I would be delighted to wash dishes tonight," it will not be received as an expression of love. On the other hand, we can share hurt, pain, and even anger in a kind manner, and that will be an expression of love. "I felt disappointed that you didn't offer to help me this evening," said in an honest, kind manner, can be an expression of love. The person speaking wants to be known by the other person and is taking steps to build authenticity into their relationship. The same words expressed with a loud, harsh voice will not be an expression of love but an expression of condemnation and judgment.

The manner in which we speak is exceedingly important. An ancient sage once said, "A gentle answer turns away wrath."[4] When your work colleague is angry and lashing with words of heat, if you choose to be loving, you will not reciprocate with additional heat but with a soft voice. You will receive what he is saying as information about his emotional feelings. You will let him tell you of his hurt, anger, and perception of events. You will seek to put yourself in his shoes and see the event through his eyes and then express softly and kindly your understanding of why he feels that way. If you have wronged him, you will be willing to confess the wrong and ask forgiveness. If your perception is different than his, you will be able to explain your point of view kindly. You will seek understanding and reconciliation and seek not to prove that your own perception is the only logical way to interpret what has happened. That is mature love. Mature love speaks kindly.

ABOUT FORGIVENESS

Processing hurt and anger in a positive way is essential if we are to speak affirming words. Typically, our words are an overflow of what is going on in our hearts. If we have not successfully dealt with hurt and anger, we will probably come out fighting, and our words will be destructive rather than loving.

None of us is perfect. We do not always do the best or right thing. We have sometimes done and said hurtful things to those around us. We cannot erase the past; we can only confess it and agree that it was wrong. We can ask for forgiveness and try to act differently in the future. Having confessed my failure and asked forgiveness, I can pursue the possibility of restitution. "Can I do something that will make up for the pain I have caused you?" is a loving question.

When I have been wronged and the person has confessed and requested forgiveness, I have the option of forgiving or demanding justice. If I choose justice and seek to pay the individual back for what he or she has done to me, I am making myself the judge and the other person the felon. If, however, I choose to forgive, then reconciliation becomes a possibility.

Many people mess up every new day with what happened yesterday. They insist on bringing into today the failures of yesterday, and in so doing pollute a potentially wonderful day. When bitterness, resentment, and revenge are allowed to live in the human heart, words of affirmation will be impossible to speak. The best thing we can do with past failures is to let them be history.

Yes, it happened. Certainly it hurt. It may still hurt. But either the person has acknowledged his or her failure and I have chosen to forgive the individual, or he/she persists in the wrong behavior and I choose to release that person to God, knowing that He is a God of justice as well as a God of mercy. I refuse to allow the other's behavior to destroy my life today.

Releasing the person is not forgiveness. Forgiveness is a response to confession. It is rather a releasing of my hurt and anger so that I am no longer consumed by them. It is choosing to love people in spite of the wrong they have done to me. It does not restore the relationship, but it does allow me to live my life in peace and love toward others.

If one wishes to be a lover, he must look carefully at the words he uses when he talks to coworkers, neighbors, close friends, parents, former spouses, roommates, and the sales clerk at the local store. What I say and the way I say it will influence the climate of my relationships. Words of affirmation enhance relationships. Harsh, condemning words destroy relationships.

Remember, love is a choice. Choose to love others.

THINGS TO THINK ABOUT

1. To what degree did you receive words of affirmation from your parents?

2. Do you find it easy or difficult to speak words of affirmation to your parents? Why?

3. If you find it difficult, is it time for you to take the initiative to express words of affirmation to your parents?

4. How freely do you express words of affirmation in other relationships?

5. Is there a relationship you would like to enhance? Do you think speaking words of affirmation would be meaningful to that person?

4

love language #2:
GIFTS

A LITTLE WHILE AGO I visited a widow who had recently moved to an assisted-living facility. During our conversation I asked how she was enjoying her new home. "It's a little tight," she said. "I had to get rid of most of my furniture.

"The kids didn't want me to bring that rocking chair," she said, pointing to a chair in the corner. "But Marvin gave that to me. I just couldn't part with it."

"Was Marvin a gift giver?" I inquired.

"Not really," she said. "In fact, that's one of the few gifts I remember him giving me. When our first child was born, he bought me that rocking chair. I had mentioned that it would be nice to have a rocking chair to nurse the baby, but I was shocked when a week later he walked in with the chair. I nursed both of our babies in that chair. I guess it's like having a little bit of Marvin and the children still with me."

"I'm glad you kept the chair," I said. "I hope you will keep it forever."

Later, as I was leaving, I glanced back at the rocking chair and knew I was looking at a gift that had communicated love for over forty years. The gift had even outlived the giver.

THE MEANING OF A GIFT

The Right Gift

A gift is a tangible object that says, "I was thinking about you. I wanted you to have this. I love you."

My academic background is anthropology—the study of cultures. Anthropologists have never discovered a culture where gift giving is not an expression of love. Giving gifts is one of the fundamental universal languages of love.

Some gifts only last for a few hours. Many moms will remember this gift—a dandelion picked from the yard and given to her by her child. The gift was quickly gone, but the memory has lingered for years. Other gifts, like the rocking chair, endure for a lifetime. The important thing is not the gift, but the emotional love that was communicated by the gift. The right gift is any token, big or small, which speaks that emotional love.

The Wrong Meaning

The Greek word from which we get our English word *gift* is *charis*, which means "grace," or an undeserved gift. A gift by its very nature is not payment for services rendered. When a dating partner says, "I will give you . . . if you will . . . " the partner is not offering a gift, nor is he expressing love. The person is simply striking a deal. A gift is given without strings attached, or it ceases to be a gift.

A gift is not a gift when it is given to smooth ruffled feathers. Some people think that giving a gift will offset the harsh words they have spoken. Some sons were instructed by their fathers, "When you've done wrong, always get her flowers. Flowers cover a multitude of sins." After a while, however, girls who receive these flowers regularly just want to throw them in the guys' face. A gift is a gift only when given as a genuine expression of love, not as an effort to cover over past failures.

Gifts are visual symbols of love. During most wedding ceremonies the bride and groom give and receive rings. The person performing the ceremony says, "These rings are outward and visible signs of an inward and spiritual bond which unite your two hearts in love that has no end."

In the original *The Five Love Languages*, I noted the significance of those words surrounding the wedding ring:

This is not meaningless rhetoric. It is verbalizing a significant truth. Symbols have emotional value. Perhaps it is more graphically displayed near the end of a disintegrating marriage. When the husband or wife stops wearing the wedding ring, it is a visual sign that the marriage is in serious trouble. One husband said, "When she threw her wedding rings at me and angrily walked out of the house slamming the door behind her, I knew our marriage was in serious trouble. I didn't pick up her rings for two days. When I finally did, I cried uncontrollably." The rings were a symbol of what should have been, but lying in his hand and not on her finger, they were visual reminders that the marriage was falling apart.[1]

The lonely rings stirred deep emotions within the husband. Many divorced individuals can identify with these deep emotions.

The gift can be any size, shape, color, or price. It may be purchased, found, or made. To the individual whose primary love language is receiving gifts, the cost of the gift won't really matter. If you can afford it, you can purchase a beautiful card for less than five dollars. If you cannot, you can make one for free. Just go get the paper out of the trash can where you work, fold it in the middle, take scissors and cut out a heart, write "I love you," and sign your name. Gifts don't need to be expensive to have meaning.

DEVELOP THE LANGUAGE OF GIFT GIVING

But what about the person who says, "I'm not a gift giver. I didn't receive many gifts growing up. I never learned how to select gifts. It doesn't come naturally for me"? Congratulations, you have just made the first discovery of becoming a great lover of people. Love requires effort. Love often requires learning a language you have never spoken. Fortunately, gift giving is one of the easiest love languages to learn.

Learn Their Interests

Where do you begin? Listen to the people you care about. Pick up on their interests or the interests of their children.

Some people are collectors. Some time ago I met a lady who had collected over a thousand salt and pepper shakers. Most of them had been given to her by friends who knew of her interest.

Bob had a secretary who was a single mom. He heard her mention one day that her twelve-year-old son collected baseball cards. He asked her to find out which cards he would like to have. Bob was on a business trip and discovered a card shop near his hotel. In five minutes he had located a baseball card on his list. After giving it to his secretary to take to her son, he said, "You would have thought I had just given her a million dollars."

It takes time and the conscious choice to listen. For most of us it also requires making a list of the ideas we hear. Otherwise we forget them before we find the gift. Some people like "country" gifts like those found at Cracker Barrel restaurants and gift shops. Other people want nothing to do with that kind of stuff. If they receive such a gift, it will go in the closet or attic. If you want your gifts to communicate love, it is best to discover the interests of the other person.

Matt and Anna had been dating for two months. She noticed that on several occasions when they were eating out he had ordered apple pie as dessert. One night she asked, "Do you like apple pie?"

"It's my favorite," he said. "I've always liked apple pie."

If Anna chooses to give him a gift, she now has an excellent clue.

In the flow of normal conversation another evening Anna shared with Matt, "Since Mom has been sick I've tried to go over and see her more often. The price of gas has really started to add up pretty quickly."

If Matt is listening, he has discovered that a prepaid gas card would be an excellent gift for Anna.

People speak about what interests them or what needs they have. If we begin to listen carefully, we will pick up all kinds of clues as to what would be appropriate gifts for the people we care about.

Be Sensitive to the Nature of Some Gifts

In a dating relationship, you must also be sensitive to the way your partner responds to gifts. Because of their cost or perceived meaning, certain types of gifts may not be readily accepted by the one you love. At a singles conference in the mountains of North Carolina, Josh approached me after a lecture on the five love languages with a perplexing question. "I believe in all five love languages, but what if you try to speak a love language and your dating partner is not willing to accept it?" he asked.

"Could you give me an example?" I requested.

"Well, I've been dating this girl for three months. I'm really excited about her. Samantha's the most wonderful person I've ever met. I wanted her to know how much I cared about her, so I bought her a really expensive gift. But when I gave it to her, she said, 'I cannot accept this. I just don't feel right about it.' I was devastated," he said.

"I still don't understand," he continued. "I really wanted her to have it."

"I think I know why she rejected the gift," I said, "but I'm not sure you will want to hear it."

"Oh, I want to hear it," he said. "I really do."

"Okay," I said, "here's my guess. I think the two of you have different ideas about the current level of your relationship. It is obvious to me that you are very interested in Samantha. You said that she is the most wonderful girl you have ever met. The fact that you would buy her such an expensive gift indicates how deeply you feel about her."

Josh was nodding his head in affirmation. So I continued, "The problem is that Samantha views the relationship differently. She obviously has an interest in the relationship or she would not be dating you, but she is not as far along as you. In her mind, it is too early in the relationship to be receiving such expensive gifts. She doesn't want to give you the wrong impression. She doesn't feel that the relationship has reached the level where she would feel comfortable in receiving such a gift as an expression of your love. Therefore, you must accept this and respect her wishes."

There was a long pause, and then Josh said, "You're right. I don't want to hear that, but I think you're right. I love her so much and I wanted to do something really nice for her. But I guess I'll have to give it more time and hope that she will come to love me as much as I love her."

I nodded and said, "Six months from now when Christmas rolls around you might test the waters before you purchase the gift. You could say something like this: 'I want to do something really nice for you this holiday, but I don't want to surprise you. Would you be willing to accept

_____ (name the gift) as an expression of my love for you? No strings attached. I just want you to know that I love you.' If she says yes, you will know the relationship has matured. If she says no, then the relationship is in trouble."

"I'll do it," he said, "and I hope by then she will receive it."

Josh learned an important lesson: You cannot force someone to accept an expression of love. You can only offer it. If it is not accepted, you must respect the other person's decision.

GIFTS AND MONEY

If you are to become an effective gift giver, you may have to change your attitude about money. Each of us has an individualized perception of the purposes of money, and we have various emotions associated with spending it. If you have a spending orientation, you will feel good about yourself when you are spending money. If you have a saving and investing perspective, you will feel good about yourself when you are saving money or investing it wisely.

Suppose you are a saver. Your emotions will resist the idea of spending money as an expression of love. I don't purchase things for myself. Why should I purchase things for others? But that attitude fails to understand the truth—that you are purchasing things for yourself. By saving and investing money you are purchasing self-worth and emotional security. You are caring for your own emotional needs in the way you handle money. If you discover that someone you care about has the primary love language of receiving gifts, then perhaps you will understand that purchasing and giving gifts to him or her is the best investment you can make. You're investing in your relationship and filling the other person's emotional love tank.

Love, Money, and Single Parents

Remember, the purpose of a gift is to emotionally communicate, "I love you. I hope this gift will enhance your life." This is extremely important for single parents (and really, all parents) to remember. Gifts should never be given simply because a child or teenager begs for them. The question should be, "Is this gift for the well-being of my teenager?"

If the answer is no, then the parent cannot conscientiously give the gift to a teenager. For example, consider the now common practice in middle-class America for many affluent parents to give their sixteen-year-old a car. I'm not suggesting this is always bad for every family. What I am suggesting is that parents need to ask the question, "Is the gift of a car a good thing for my teenager?"

In answering that question parents must weigh a couple of factors. One is the level of maturity and responsibility of the teenager himself. Just because the state says they can legally drive doesn't mean everyone is emotionally ready for a car at age sixteen. Some teens have not demonstrated a sufficient level of responsibility in other areas that merit the giving of a car.

A second factor is the financial ability of a single parent to provide a car. Overly committing yourself financially to give such a gift to a teenager is not ultimately good for them or for you.

While I'm talking to single parents, let me say a word to some other parents, usually fathers (sorry dads), who try to make up for their failures by lavishing unnecessary gifts on their children. There is one kind of gift that no teenager needs. It is what I call the counterfeit gift. This is the gift—often gifts—designed to take the place of true love. Such gifts are given by busy and sometimes absentee parents who are caught up in the busyness of life and have little time for speaking the love languages of words of affirmation and the remaining three languages of love: quality time, acts of service, and physical touch. So they try to make up for this deficit by giving the teenager extraneous gifts.

One single mom said, "Every time my sixteen-year-old goes to visit her father, she comes home with a suitcase full of gifts. He is not willing to help me with her medical and dental bills, but he always has money for gifts. He seldom calls her on the phone and only spends two weeks in the summer with her. But somehow the gifts are supposed to make everything all right."

This kind of gift giving on the part of non-involved parents has become commonplace. The teenager typically receives the gifts, expresses verbal appreciation, and goes home with an empty love tank. When gifts are given as a substitute for genuine love, the teenager sees them as the shallow counterfeit they are.

RECOGNIZING GIFTS AS SOMEONE'S PRIMARY LANGUAGE

For some people, receiving gifts is their primary love language. It is what makes them feel loved most deeply. Amanda, who had been dating Ben for nine months, was very vulnerable when she said, "I want you to know that birthdays and special holidays are very important to me. I remember crying for two days when my father forgot my sixteenth birthday. I knew he didn't love my mother; that's why he left. But on my birthday, I found out he didn't love me either."

If Ben has been listening, he has just discovered that Amanda's primary love language is gifts. If he wants her to feel loved, he will not only remember birthdays and other holidays, but he will give her gifts on a hot August day and a chilly January afternoon — anytime, for no special reason, just to express his love. These "no strings attached" gifts mean the most and have the greatest impact.

The single-parent dad who picks up a stone while hiking a mountain trail and gives it to his ten-year-old son might discover it in his dresser drawer when the son is twenty-three years old if his boy's primary love language is receiving gifts. The gift said, "Daddy was thinking of me." Every time he sees the stone he thinks of his father and feels loved.

Gifts need not be expensive; after all, "it's the thought that counts." But I remind you, it is not the thought left in your head that counts; it is the gift that came out of the thought that communicates emotional love.

Bridget's Teddy Bears

Chris had been dating Bridget for about six months when he made an appointment to see me. He was very straightforward about the purpose of his visit. "Bridget and I have been dating for six months. Things are going really well. I really like her, but there's one thing that bothers me. She has at least fifty teddy bears in her bedroom. Half of them are on her bed. She sleeps with them. I could understand that if she were six years old, but I don't understand it now that she's twenty-six. She even has names for most of them. It's like they are her children.

"This seems strange to me, and I don't know how this would work if we ever got married. I'm not into sleeping with teddy bears. So what I want to know is, am I missing something, or is this normal behavior for a twenty-six-year-old girl?"

Chris was smiling, so I smiled and decided to keep things on the lighter side for a moment. So I said, "If by normal you mean, do all twenty-six-year-old single girls sleep with a room full of teddy bears, the answer is no. Some sleep with live dogs, and others have fish in their bedrooms. I even know one gal who has snakes, in cages mind you, but nonetheless snakes in her bedroom."

Chris interrupted. "I don't think I'd be dating that girl," he said. We both laughed. Then I turned the conversation to a more serious note.

"What is important, Chris, is not what a girl has in her bedroom, but the emotional significance of the things in her bedroom." I could see the question marks forming in Chris's eyes.

"Then this is more serious than I thought," he said.

"Not necessarily," I responded. "Let me ask you some questions. You mentioned that Bridget had given most of the teddy bears names. Do you know where the teddy bears came from?"

"Most of them were gifts," he said. "In fact, she knows who gave her each of the bears—and when. It seems that her parents have given her a teddy bear every birthday since she was a child. So that accounts for about half of them. Some of the others were given by aunts and uncles and a few by her younger brother.

"She even has two that were given by former boyfriends. Frankly, those really bug me," Chris said. I nodded approvingly because it was pretty obvious that Chris felt strongly about those two bears.

"I think I know what's going on," I said, "but I'm not sure you want to hear it."

"Is it bad?" he asked.

"No," I said. "As a matter of fact, it's good."

"Then I want to hear it," Chris said. I knew Chris was listening, so I proceeded.

"It seems to me that Bridget's primary love language is gifts. Gifts speak deeply to her. What do you think is your primary love language? What makes you feel most loved?"

"Words of affirmation," he said quickly. "Maybe that's why I like Bridget so much. She's always giving me affirming words."

"That makes a lot of sense," I said. "Now what I'm suggesting is that Bridget's primary love language is gifts. That's why she remembers who gave her each of the bears. That's why she gave them all names. That's why she keeps them in her bedroom. Every bear says, 'I love you.'"

"Yeah, but those two from her boyfriends, they need to go, right? I mean, I don't want to date her and have two other guys saying 'I love you' every night." I laughed, but I could tell Chris was serious.

"Yes," I replied, "if your relationship with Bridget becomes more of a long-term thing, there will be a time when those two bears need to find another home. But if you're going to continue to date Bridget, you need to fall in love with teddy bears. In fact, you now know what to give her on the first anniversary of the beginning of your relationship or for her birthday if that comes first.

"To insist that she get rid of the teddy bears is to insist that she spurn the love of her mother, father, aunts, uncles, and younger brother. It would be like asking you to use disparaging words toward your own mom and dad and the significant people in your life. That's too much to ask. In fact, you don't want to marry a girl who turns against the love of parents and relatives." Chris was nodding as though he understood, so I continued.

"You see, Chris, it's not the teddy bears to which she is attached. It's the love behind the teddy bears. Her parents could just as easily have given her stuffed rabbits each year, or frogs."

"I'm just glad they didn't give her snakes," Chris said.

"Teddy bears *are* pretty mild," I said.

"Yeah, I'm starting to fall in love with teddy bears already," Chris said, smiling.

"Now, please don't hear me saying that you must give her a teddy bear for every anniversary. One teddy bear from you is probably enough. Then you can branch out to give other gifts. But what I am saying is that gifts are very significant to Bridget. It is her primary love language. A gift says to her, 'He was thinking about me. He loves me.'" I reminded him that gifts need not be expensive, but a rose or even her favorite candy bar could speak volumes.

"I've never been much of a gift giver," Chris said. "Gifts are really not very important to me."

"Then it will take time and effort for you to learn to speak this love language," I said, "but it is essential if you want your relationship with Bridget to flourish. All of us blossom when we feel loved and wither when we do not feel loved. The reason Bridget is so positive and excited about life is that she has felt loved by the significant people in her life. You don't want to diminish that; you want to add to that."

Earlier in our conversation I mentioned to Chris that I was writing a book on the five love languages for singles. As he left my office, he said, "Oh, by the way, when you finish that book I want to buy the first copy."

"I'll make sure you get one," I said, "but don't wait until the book is published before you start loving teddy bears."

"Oh, I'm going to be the greatest teddy bear lover you've ever seen," he said as he walked away with a smile.

Two months later I met Bridget at a Fourth of July celebration. Chris introduced her to me, and she said, "I want to thank you for the time you spent with Chris. He told me what you shared with him, and it made so much sense to me. I had never thought of it that way. I didn't realize my primary love language was gifts, but it's really true. Incidentally," she said, holding up her hand, "this is the friendship ring that Chris gave me last week."

"Oooh," I said, "Chris is a fast learner."

"I don't know how fast I am," Chris said, "but I know that I love Bridget and I want her to feel loved."

Fireworks . . . and a Thumbs-Up

"And is Bridget speaking your love language?" I asked.

"Absolutely! She gives me words of affirmation all the time," Chris said.

"I think I'm lucky," Bridget said, "because speaking words of affirmation is easy for me. I love people. I guess I learned it growing up. My parents were always very affirming."

"Maybe words of affirmation is your secondary love language," I said to Bridget. "Do you also like to receive affirming words?"

"Oh yeah," she said, "and Chris does a great job with that."

"I predict a long and satisfying relationship for you two," I said as the fireworks began to light the sky.

As Chris walked away he looked back over his shoulder and holding up two fingers said, "Two teddy bears are gone!" I smiled and nodded.

Bridget heard what he said, stopped, and turned to me, saying, "I gave them to the Salvation Army. Hopefully someone else will feel loved when they receive them." I gave her a thumbs-up as they walked away.

Chris and Bridget illustrate the kind of conflicts that arise in dating relationships when individuals do not understand love languages. Chris simply found it odd that a twenty-six-year-old woman would have a bedroom filled with teddy bears. It seemed abnormal to him. However, when he understood that receiving gifts is one of the five primary love languages, and that the teddy bears were gifts from significant people in her life, it all made sense to him.

Please don't hear me saying that you speak only the primary love language of the people you care for. Love can be expressed and received in all five languages. However, if you don't speak a person's primary love language, that person will not feel loved, even though you may be speaking the other four. Once you are speaking his or her primary love language fluently, then you can sprinkle in the other four, and they will be like icing on the cake.

THINGS TO THINK ABOUT

1. To what degree was the love language of gifts spoken by your parents to you and to each other?

2. How often do you give gifts to those you love and care for?

3. What is the last gift you gave and to whom did you give it?

4. Do you find speaking the love language of gifts difficult, or does it come naturally for you? Why?

5. In your conversation with others, do you consciously listen for gift ideas? Would keeping a gift list in your notebook be helpful for you?

6. If you enjoy receiving gifts, from whom would you most like to receive one? Would it be appropriate for you to give this person a gift this week?

5

love language #3:
ACTS OF SERVICE

JENNY ENTERED the workforce after her husband left her and her four-year-old daughter. Her computer skills are not as advanced as she would like, but she is improving. She also has a very helpful coworker who has made the transition as a single mother in the workplace much easier.

"Beth is so nice," Jenny told me. "Whenever I have a problem with my computer, she's always available to help me. She is so patient when I am slow to learn. She is the greatest! I don't know what I'd do without her."

Jenny has high positive regard for Beth because her coworker is speaking Jenny's primary love language: acts of service.

Albert Einstein, one of history's greatest scientists, is best known for his theory of relativity, which he advanced in 1905 at the age of twenty-six. He made many other significant contributions to science. However, in his later years, he is said to have removed from his walls the portraits of two scientists, Maxwell and Newton, and replaced them with the portraits of Schweitzer and Gandhi. When questioned by his colleagues, he answered, "It is time to remove the symbols of science and replace them with the symbols of service."[1]

Apparently Einstein had come to realize that love is more powerful than science. One of the fundamental languages of love is acts of service. One of the clearest pictures of the essence of the Christian faith is that of Jesus washing the feet of His disciples. In a culture where people wore sandals and walked on dirt streets, it was customary for the servant of the household to wash the generally gross and grimy feet of guests as they arrived. Jesus, who had instructed His disciples to love one another, gave them an example of how to express that love when He took a basin and a towel and proceeded to wash their feet. After that simple expression of love, He encouraged His disciples to follow His example.[2]

Earlier in His life Jesus had indicated that in His kingdom those who would be great would be servants. In most societies those who are great lord it over those who are small, but Jesus said that those who are great would serve others. The apostle Paul summarized that philosophy when he said, "Serve one another in love."[3]

In our "Me Generation" the idea of service may seem anachronistic, but the life of service to others has always been recognized as a life worthy of emulation. In every vocation, those who truly excel have a genuine desire to serve others. The most notable physicians view their vocation as a calling to serve the sick and diseased. Truly great political leaders see themselves as "public servants." The greatest of all educators see students as individuals and gain their greatest rewards from seeing students reach their potential in developing their talents and interests. Service to others is our greatest aspiration.

SERVICE VERSUS SLAVERY

Let me quickly clarify the difference between service and slavery. Slavery is at the heart of dysfunctional families. When people serve others because they are forced to do so, freedom to truly serve is lost. Slavery hardens the heart. Slavery creates anger, bitterness, and resentment.

Listen to the emotional pain of a divorced single: "I served him for twenty years. I have waited on him hand and foot. I have been his doormat while he ignored me, mistreated me, and humiliated me in front of my friends and family. I don't hate him. I wish him no ill, but I resent him and I no longer wish to live with him." That wife has performed acts of service for twenty years, but they have not been expressions of love. They were done out of fear, guilt, and resentment.

A doormat is an inanimate object. You can wipe your feet on it, step on it, kick it around, or do whatever you like with it. It has no will of its own. It can be your servant, but not your lover. When you treat another person as an object, you preclude the possibility of love. Manipulation by guilt ("If you loved me, you would do this for me") is not the language of love. Coercion by fear ("You will do this or you will be sorry") has no place in love.

No person should ever be a doormat. We are creatures of emotion, thoughts, and desires. We have the ability to make decisions and take action. Allowing oneself to be used or manipulated by another is not an act of love. It is, in fact, an act of treason. You are allowing the person who is manipulating you to develop inhumane habits. Love says, "I love you too much to let you treat me this way. It is not good for you or me." Love refuses to be manipulated.

On the other hand, true love often finds its expression in acts of service. It is service freely given, not out of fear, but out of choice. It comes out of the personal discovery that "it is more blessed to give than to receive."[4] All of us have certain abilities and skills. These can be used to express love. This is how Beth used her computer skills to express love to Jenny.

THE MANY ACTS OF SERVICE

Of course, acts of service do not require highly technical skills. A number of years ago my wife and I opened our house on Friday evenings to young singles who had recently moved to our city and had been visiting our church. It was not a highly structured evening, but rather a place where singles could ask questions, meet people, and develop relationships. After one of these evenings, one young man stayed behind and said to me, "These meetings are so meaningful and so helpful. I really would like to do something to show you and Mrs. Chapman how much I appreciate your opening your home to us. I was wondering if one night this week I might come over and clean your oven?" (This was in the days before we had a "self-cleaning" oven.)

Karolyn and I had both done the spray-and-chip project. I knew how much she hated it, and to be honest, it was not my favorite job either. So I said without hesitation, "That would be wonderful." Later that week he came over and cleaned our oven while Karolyn and I took the children out for an evening of fun. We returned to a sparkling clean oven.

That happened more than thirty years ago. The young man has long since moved from our community, but neither of us has ever forgotten his name and his act of kindness.

Life is filled with opportunities to express love by acts of service. You accompany a coworker to the parking lot and find her left front tire flat. An older single adult needs a ride to the doctor's office or to church. You have a date for the evening—why not call ahead and ask if she needs a loaf of bread or some milk, which you can pick up on your way over? (If you pay for it, it is both a gift and an act of service.) Taking your elderly mother to the grocery store is an act of service.

For some singles this love language comes easy. They grew up in homes where they were taught that "actions speak louder than words."

They were praised when they did acts of service for family members, and the family often did service projects for the elderly or those in need. They feel deeply that to love means to serve. Consequently they are alert to the opportunities around them.

A DIFFICULT LANGUAGE FOR SOME

Others will find this love language extremely difficult to speak because their family of origin emphasized everyone fending for himself. "Don't expect me to take care of you all the time" is the message those people heard during their childhoods. Consequently, the focus of their lives is looking out for their own needs. They expect everyone else to do the same. *Why should I do something for others they can do for themselves?* is their way of thinking. "Oh, sure, I would help a little old lady in need," he says. But in reality he seldom does.

If you happen to be rooming or working with a person with this orientation, you had better ask before you give her (or him) an act of service. If you clean her bathroom while she is away, she may be offended. *She thinks I wasn't doing my job* is likely the thought that will run through her mind. To you it was an act of love, but to her it was an insult.

Therefore, before doing an act of service, you'd better ask, "Would it be helpful to you if I did _____." After all, your purpose is to enhance their life by expressing love. You don't want to do something that the person will interpret negatively. If her response is "No, I'd rather do that myself," don't take it as a personal rejection. She's simply informing you that she doesn't want to receive that love language at the moment.

However, if acts of service do not come naturally for you, it is still a love language worth acquiring. It is a way of expressing a sense of responsibility for the well-being of others. Albert Schweitzer said repeatedly, "As long as there is a man in the world who is hungry, sick, lonely or living in fear, he is my responsibility."[5] Helping others is universally accepted as an expression of love.

A REALLY BIG UMBRELLA

Leah was one of several single adults who attended my marriage seminar in Cleveland. She explained, "I just want to learn more about marriage so that if I ever get married I'll know what I'm supposed to do." I wish more singles had that attitude before they got married. After lunch she asked if she could speak with me.

"I don't want to take too much time," she said, "but I have a problem." I nodded and she continued.

"I've been dating a man for about six months who is the most wonderful man in the world, but I don't have romantic feelings for him. I wish I did because he's so wonderful."

"So what makes you think he is so wonderful?" I asked.

"He is the nicest man I have ever met. I've never had a man do so much for me."

"What does he do for you?" I asked.

"Well, it all started one night at church," she said. "I had been to a singles meeting, and when I got ready to leave the church it was raining really hard. He stepped up with this huge umbrella and asked if he could take me to the car. I never remember having seen him before, but he said he had been attending about three weeks. Well, of course I accepted his offer. He got me to my car and told me to have a good evening. I thanked him; he closed the door and then walked to his car. I was appreciative, but it wasn't a big deal.

"I didn't think of him again until I noticed him in the singles meeting two weeks later. Afterward he asked me if I would like to get a milkshake. A milkshake sounded great to me, so I accepted. We walked across the street to the ice cream shop. I found out that he had never been married, was an electrical engineer who worked for a local company, and had lived in Cleveland about two years, having been transferred from back East. I enjoyed talking with him. However, when we got ready to leave it was raining again. He told me to wait while he got his car, then he would give me a ride to my car. Not wanting to get my hair wet, I agreed.

"He ran across the street and returned shortly with his car, met me at the door with the umbrella, then drove me to my car. He was soaking wet. As I drove home I had the thought that he's a really nice guy, but I certainly didn't think about dating him.

"Well, about three weeks later I ran into him at the singles gathering. Earlier that afternoon, I was having trouble with my computer. As I explained it, he said he thought he could fix it pretty quickly. If I would like, he would follow me home and fix it. So I agreed. He figured out the problem pretty quickly, but needed a part or something, so he went back to his house and about forty-five minutes later returned and fixed my computer within five minutes.

"I offered him a Coke, and we chatted about the computer for a few minutes. I told him how much I appreciated him helping me and offered to pay him. He refused and said that he was happy he could help me."

Like someone right out of classic literature, the man was seemingly always ready to help. At a later singles meeting, he told Leah about a computer program he thought would be helpful for her.

"I'd be glad to install it if you would like."

After he explained what it did, Leah agreed and invited him over to install it.

"He showed me how it worked, and I realized that it was going to help me out a lot," Leah explained. "So again I offered to pay him and expressed appreciation. He refused to accept anything and told me again he was glad that he could help me.

"To make a long story short," she said (by this time I was really glad to hear those words), "we started going out to eat about once a week, and he started coming over to my place and helping me with various fix-it projects. He trimmed the door to my closet so I could get it closed. He put a dead bolt lock on my front door. He helped me get a couple of windows unjammed. He showed me how to replace the filter in my furnace. He helped me figure out how to use some of the features on my new cell phone. He fixed my toaster when it started burning everything.

"I mean, this man is just incredible! I want him to be in my life forever, but I don't have romantic feelings for him, and physically I'm not attracted to him. I don't think I should marry him, but I really like having him around."

"Do you think he has romantic feelings for you?" I asked.

"I don't know," she said. "We've never talked about it. He hasn't tried to kiss me, he doesn't put his arm around my shoulder, and we don't hold hands. It's just like a really good friendship. But I want to date other people, not anyone in particular, I mean, I really want to be romantically involved with somebody, and I don't know if this can happen as long as I'm seeing him. But I don't want to hurt him either. He's been so nice to me. I don't know what to do."

LEAH'S DAD

I had the feeling that Leah was asking for the wisdom of Solomon. Since I was not Solomon, I continued asking questions, "I'm going to change the subject for a moment, okay?" She nodded and I continued. "When you were growing up, was your father a handyman around the house?"

"Oh, yes. He did all the painting, all the repairs. If anything went wrong, Daddy could fix it. In fact, he fixed things for the whole neighborhood. When I got my first car as a teenager, it seemed like every week something went wrong, but Dad always fixed it. When I went to college there was some problem with the electrical system in my dorm room. I tried to get the maintenance people to fix it, but when they didn't respond, eventually Dad came and fixed it."

"How would you describe your relationship with your father?" I asked.

"Oh, Dad and I were always close. I am very fortunate to have had a dad who really loved me."

"How do you know he loved you?" I asked.

"Well, like I said, all the things he did for me. He was always there when I needed him."

"Do you see any similarities between your father and the man you're dating?" I inquired.

Leah pondered a moment and then said, "Yes, now that you mention it, I do. Actually, Mark is doing all the things that Dad used to do. He's a good man, just like my dad. But I don't want to marry my dad," she said. She was now smiling and wiping a tear from her eye at the same time.

"I think I can explain what is going on," I said. "Do you remember the lecture I gave before lunch on the five love languages?"

"Yes," she said. "I thought it was very insightful."

"Well, my guess is that your primary love language is acts of service. You felt loved by your father because he spoke your love language." Leah was nodding. "And you feel loved by Mark because he's also speaking your primary love language."

"But what about the romantic feelings?" Leah interrupted.

"I'm coming to that, but first of all, I want you to understand why you feel so close to Mark, why you value his friendship, and why you think he's such a wonderful person.

"When someone speaks our primary love language, we are drawn to them emotionally. We have high, positive regard for them. We want to do something that will enhance their lives and reciprocate their love to us. That is likely why you started dating Mark. His acts of kindness to you stimulated a desire in you to do something kind for him. So, even though you felt no romantic feelings for him and were not attracted to him physically, it still seemed the natural thing to do. Now you have developed a loving, kind friendship and you don't want to hurt Mark, yet you want to have a romantic relationship with someone else. So, you are caught in the middle."

SUGGESTIONS FOR LEAH

"That's exactly where I am. What am I going to do?"

"Well, I can't tell you what to do, but I can share some ideas that might help you decide what you ought to do.

"First, you must speak the truth to yourself. You are speaking it to me today, but you've got to be honest with yourself. The truth is you have a friendship that is very meaningful to you because Mark is speaking your primary love language. But this is not a romantic relationship that might lead to marriage. Consequently, there is the real possibility that if and when you develop a romantic relationship with someone else, this friendship will certainly diminish and perhaps cease to exist." Leah agreed with my conclusion, so I continued.

"Then the second idea is this . . . " I realized that in Leah's emotional state she may not remember anything I was about to say, so I asked, "Would you like to write these ideas down?" handing her my pen. "Oh, yes," she said, reaching for her purse to find paper.

"The second idea," I repeated, "is to find out what is going on inside Mark's head. What does he feel about his relationship with you? Does he have romantic feelings for you? You can't possibly make a wise decision without having this information."

"But how do I find out?" she said.

"The best way is to ask him," I replied.

"But I can't just say, 'Do you have romantic feelings for me?'"

"No, but you can say something like, 'Mark, I've been thinking about our friendship, and I'm feeling the need to find out if we are on the same page. So I'm going to be vulnerable and share with you how I view our relationship, and then I'm going to ask you to do the same. Is this a good time for us to have this conversation?'

"Then if he agrees, you proceed. You could say something like this: 'First of all, I really value our friendship. I hope it can continue. You have been so kind to me, and I really enjoy our times together, but I don't view it as a romantic relationship.'"

"Just a minute, let me write that down," she said. So I repeated it as she wrote it down.

"'I think you deserve to know that. The last thing I want to do is hurt you, but I do think you deserve the truth. Maybe I'm being silly to talk about this, but I just want to make sure that we understand each other. Does that make sense?' Then you listen carefully to Mark's response; ask clarifying questions so that you are sure you understand where he is and go from there."

I continued, "If he sees the relationship as you see it, a nonromantic friendship, then you can continue the friendship, and he will give you the freedom to date someone else. If, on the other hand, he has strong romantic feelings for you, the thought of dating someone else while maintaining a friendship with him might not be possible. But at least you'll know the facts, and you can make your decision accordingly. He may choose to end the relationship. Or, if he has romantic feelings for you and realizes that you don't have anyone in particular that you want to date at the moment, he may ask to continue the relationship until you meet someone that you'd like to date. The two of you agree that at that time Mark will have the option of walking out of your life. If he does not have romantic feelings for you, then he may be happy for you to have the freedom to develop a romantic relationship with someone else while remaining a friend of his, as long as that does not interfere with your new relationship."

Our time was gone. It was almost time for me to start my next seminar session. Leah expressed appreciation and joined her group of friends for the rest of the seminar. When the seminar was over Leah thanked me again.

I nodded, accepting her appreciation for our time together, and said, "I only have one further comment. I hope that the person with whom you develop a romantic relationship and whom you will eventually marry speaks the love language of acts of service. If he does, it will make life a lot easier for him. If he doesn't, I hope you will teach him to speak it before you get married and that he will understand why that is so important."

"Oh, I'm going to bring him to one of your seminars. I'll get him fixed up before we get married," she said, laughing as she walked away.

I never saw Leah after that seminar, but I know she recognized her primary love language and its importance to her. However, most singles do not understand the importance of the five love languages and the role of their own primary love language before they get married. They enter marriage on the excitement of the "in love" obsession, thinking it will last forever. They become disillusioned when they come down off the high and wonder what happened to their emotional love. When we learn to speak each other's love language early in our relationships, we are able to keep each other's love tanks full.

THINGS TO THINK ABOUT

1. Did your father speak the love language acts of service similar to Leah's father? What about your mother?

2. How freely do you express acts of service to others?

3. What acts of service have you done for your parents in the last three months?

4. What acts of service have you shown toward a friend or someone with whom you have a dating relationship?

5. What acts of service have others done for you recently?

6. On a scale of 0 to 10, how much love do you feel when people express acts of service to you?

7. Would you be willing to set a goal of speaking the love language acts of service at least once a week to someone you care about?

6

love language #4:
QUALITY TIME

MIKE AND JENNA HAVE been dating for six months, but Mike is extremely frustrated with their relationship. "I really like Jenna. I think we could have a good relationship. The problem is she's just not available. Her work is so demanding that she never has time for me. I get tired just sitting at home while she's gone on another business trip."

Mike is revealing his desire for quality time. The central desire of quality time is togetherness. I do not mean proximity. Two people sitting in the same room are certainly in close proximity, but they are not necessarily together. Togetherness has to do with focused attention. It is giving someone your undivided attention. As humans, we have a fundamental desire to connect with others. We may be in the presence of people all day long, but we do not always feel connected.

Physician Albert Schweitzer said, "We are all so much together, but we are all dying of loneliness."[1] Professor Leo Buscaglia notes, "There seems to be accumulating evidence that there is actually an inborn need for this togetherness, this human interaction, this love. It seems that without these close ties with other human beings, a newborn infant, for example, can regress developmentally, lose consciousness, fall into idiocy and die."[2]

When quality time is used as a means of expressing genuine love, it is a powerful emotional communicator. The single mom sitting on the floor rolling a ball to her two-year-old is giving the child quality time. For that brief moment, however long it lasts, they are together. If, however, the mother is talking on the phone while she rolls the ball, her attention is diluted. The child no longer has her undivided attention.

Quality time does not mean we must spend all of our moments gazing into each other's eyes. It may mean doing something together that we both enjoy. The particular activity is secondary, only a means to creating the sense of togetherness. The important thing about a mother rolling the ball to her two-year-old is not the activity itself, but the emotions that are created between the mother and her child. Similarly, a dating couple playing tennis together, if it is genuine quality time, will focus not on the game but on the fact that they are spending time together. What happens on the emotional level is what matters. Their spending time together in a common pursuit communicates that they care about each other, that they enjoy being with each other.

If, on the other hand, your dating partner has expressed a desire to learn to play tennis and you, being more proficient, agree to give him a tennis lesson, the focus is on developing your partner's skills. This may be an expression of love, but it's not quality time, this would be the love language known as acts of service. You are providing a desired service, teaching your partner to improve his tennis game. He may feel genuinely loved by your efforts, especially if his primary love language is acts of service. In this context, you might also speak the love language of quality time if after the instruction you sit down for a cool glass of lemonade and have a quality conversation.

DIALECTS OF QUALITY TIME: QUALITY CONVERSATION

Like *words of affirmation*, the love language of quality time also has many dialects. One of the most common dialects is that of quality conversation. By quality conversation, I mean sympathetic dialogue where two individuals are sharing their experiences, thoughts, feelings, and desires in a friendly, uninterrupted context.

Hearing . . .

Quality conversation is quite different from the love language *words of affirmation*. Affirming words focus on what we are saying, whereas quality conversation focuses more on what we are hearing. If I am sharing my love for you by means of quality time and we are going to spend that time in conversation, it means I will focus on drawing you out by listening sympathetically to what you have to say. I will ask questions, not in a badgering manner but with genuine intentions to understand your thoughts, feelings, and desires.

If I invest thirty minutes in such a conversation with you, I have given you thirty minutes of my life. Quality conversation communicates that I care. This is especially true if your primary love language is quality time.

. . . and Talking

Of course, conversation also involves talking. Many single adults (and many married ones as well) have not developed the communication skills that are necessary for quality conversations. Sarah, a woman in her late twenties, was in my office because she was having trouble in her dating relationships. Her present boyfriend had recently told her that he thought it was time for them to "go their separate ways" because their personalities were "just too different."

"His main complaint," she said, "is that I don't talk enough. I know

89

I'm rather shy," Sarah said. "I guess it goes back to my childhood. In our home, my father said, 'Children are to be seen, not heard.' He didn't make time for me or for my brother. Consequently, none of us really said much to each other at all. My mother was always busy, and my brother and I didn't get along very well. So I spent most of my childhood alone. In high school and college I focused on my studies and did well. After college, I got a job as a CPA, which requires me to be alone most of the time. I didn't realize I had a problem until I started dating. Robert is the fourth guy who has broken up with me because I don't talk enough. So, I guess I have a problem."

I knew that Sarah had a long road to walk. The pattern of solitude that she described would not be overcome in a day or two. Since she did not live in my city, I encouraged her to see a local counselor and tell him or her exactly what she had told me. I assured her that she could learn to communicate, and that if she would get counseling, a year from now she could experience a major difference in her communication patterns.

The process for Sarah, and others like her, begins with learning to get in touch with our emotions, thoughts, and desires. It is very important to get in touch with what we are experiencing each day. Then we must learn to verbalize these, first to ourselves and then to others. It is the process of re-socializing: going back and replacing the dysfunctional patterns of childhood with healthy patterns of communication. It's not easy, but necessary, if one is to learn to speak the love language of quality conversation.

DIALECTS OF QUALITY TIME: QUALITY LISTENING

Other people who talk too freely may have an equally difficult problem. They are extremely poor listeners. They listen only long enough to get the topic of your conversation, and then they proceed to tell you all the thoughts in their mind regarding that topic. Or, if you present them with a personal struggle, they will quickly move to give you an answer by telling you what you ought to do in that situation. They are adept at analyzing problems and creating solutions. But they are not adept at sympathetic listening with a view to understanding the other person.

Carol's Fear

Carol had been divorced for five years. She had been deeply involved in raising her two children, but six months ago she met Eric and, to use her words, "things have moved quickly."

"The problem is," she said, "I'm beginning to realize that Eric is a lot like my former husband. This scares me."

"In what ways is he like your former spouse?" I asked.

"Well, Daniel, my former husband, was what I call 'a fix-it man.' He always had the answer to everything. No matter what I presented, he could tell me what I ought to do about it. If I shared a problem at work, he would immediately tell me what I should say to my supervisor. If I wanted to talk about the same problem the next night, he would ask me if I talked to my supervisor. If I said no, he would say, 'Then I don't want to talk about it. When you do what I told you to do, then I'm willing to talk about it again.'

"It's like he was 'the answer man.' I needed his support and encouragement. I didn't need his know-it-all attitude.

"Now as I'm opening up to Eric, I'm beginning to see he has that same tendency. Is this true of all men?"

I could tell that Carol was beginning to wonder if she should continue her relationship with Eric.

"No," I said, "not all men are like Daniel and Eric, but I'm glad that you are being honest with yourself about what you are seeing in Eric. Are there other aspects of your relationship with Eric that you find trouble-some?" I asked.

"No," she said, "in every other way he's just wonderful. I guess that's why I'm so concerned about this one aspect of our relationship. I know how destructive it was in my marriage."

"Then, since you value the relationship, I think it's worth some time and effort to see if Eric can learn to become a sympathetic listener, rather than an answer man."

Is it Possible to Become a Sympathetic Listener?

I told Carol that I was going to be teaching a class in two weeks on "The Awesome Power of the Listening Ear." I suggested that she and Eric attend as a first step in dealing with this issue.

Here are some of the practical ideas I shared in that class. They are designed to help you become a sympathetic listener:

1. *Maintain eye contact when you are listening to someone.* This keeps your mind from wandering and communicates that the person has your full attention. Refrain from rolling your eyes in disgust, closing your eyes when they give you a low blow, looking over their head, or staring at their shoes while they are talking.

2. *Don't engage in other activities while you are listening to another individual.* Remember, quality time is giving someone your undivided attention. If you are watching, reading, or doing something else and cannot give them your attention immediately, tell the person the truth. A positive approach might be "I know you are trying to talk to me and I am very interested, but I want to give you my full attention. I can't do that right now, but if you will give me ten minutes to finish this, I'll sit down and listen to you." Most people will respect such a request.

3. *Listen for feelings.* Ask yourself: "What are this person's emotions

right now?" When you think you have the answer, confirm it. For example, "It sounds like you are feeling disappointed because I forgot . . . " That gives the person a chance to clarify his/her feelings. It also communicates that you are listening intently to what they are saying.

4. *Observe body language.* Clenched fists, trembling hands, tears, furrowed brows, and eye movement may give you clues as to what the person is feeling. Sometimes body language speaks one message while words speak another. Ask for clarification to make sure you know what the person is really thinking and feeling. For example, you might say, "I notice that you are crying while you are saying you hope he never comes back again. Does this mean that you have ambivalent feelings? Does a part of you want to see him and another part of you never want to see him again?"

5. *Refuse to interrupt.* Be careful not to interrupt someone to interject your own ideas. Such interruptions often stop the conversation before it can start. At this point in the conversation your objective is not to defend yourself or to set the other person straight. It is to understand the person's thoughts, feelings, and desires. When you interrupt too early, you may never discover what the person was really trying to say.

6. *Ask reflective questions.* When you think you understand what the person is saying, check it out by reflecting the statement back (as you understand it) in a question: "What I hear you saying is . . . Is that correct?" or, "Are you saying . . . ?" Reflective listening clears up misunderstandings and allows you to confirm (or correct) your perception of what the person is saying.

7. *Express understanding.* The person needs to know that he/she has been heard and understood. Suppose Carol discusses with Eric a problem that she is struggling through at work. What he might say is, "What I hear you saying is that you feel you are being taken advantage of by your

supervisor, that he expects you to work overtime without pay, and that he expresses little appreciation for your dedication to the job. Is that what you're feeling?" If Carol responds, "Yes, that's exactly what I'm feeling," then Eric can express understanding. "I can see how you would feel that way. If I were in your shoes, I'm sure I would feel the same way." In expressing understanding, Eric is affirming Carol's sense of worth, treating her as a person who has legitimate feelings.

8. *Ask if there is anything you might do that would be helpful.* Notice, you are asking, not telling the person what she ought to do. If Eric asks Carol, "Is there anything I can do to help?" she might say, "Just give me a hug." She doesn't want him to give her a "fix-it" answer. She already knows the answer. She just wants him to be supportive. On the other hand, if she says, "What do you think I ought to do?" then Eric is free to share his ideas. Never give advice until you are sure the other person wants it.

Obviously quality conversations like these will take time — and, to be completely honest, a good deal of effort. In fact, twice as much time will be spent listening as opposed to talking. The dividends, however, are enormous. The other person feels respected, understood, and loved, which is the goal of quality conversations.

After the class, I met Eric. Later he and I spent four counseling sessions together. At the end of the final session he said, "I want to thank you for helping me learn to be a listener. I didn't even know I had a problem until I went to your class. I always thought I was helping people by offering my advice freely. Now I understand that advice is seen as an effort to control unless it is desired by the other person. I know this is going to make a difference in my relationship with Carol, and all my other relationships as well." What Eric learned is a lesson that many singles need to learn.

DIALECTS OF QUALITY TIME: QUALITY ACTIVITIES

The basic love language of quality time has another dialect: quality activities. At a recent singles event I asked those present to complete the following sentence: "I feel most loved and appreciated by _____ when _____." They could insert the name of anyone: parent, roommate, coworker, or friend.

One twenty-seven-year-old male inserted the name of his girlfriend and completed the sentence as follows: "I feel most loved by Megan when she and I do things together—things I like to do and things she likes to do. We talk more when we're doing things. I had never ridden a horse until I met her, and she had never been sailing. I've always enjoyed doing things with other people. It's so neat to be dating someone who is open to trying new things together."

This young man was revealing that his primary love language is quality time, and the dialect he enjoys most is quality activities. The emphasis is on being together, doing things together, and giving each other undivided attention.

Quality activities may include anything in which one or both of you has an interest. The emphasis is not on what you are doing but on why you are doing it. The purpose is to experience something together, to walk away from it feeling: *He cares about me, he was willing to do something with me that I enjoy, and he did it with a positive attitude.* That is love, and for some people, it is love's loudest voice.

Entering into the Other Person's Interests

Rick grew up on country music. He never actually attended a concert, but the radio was always on and it was always tuned to the country station. For quite some time his dream was to attend the Grand Ole Opry. After he finished high school, he went to the local technical college and trained to be a computer analyst. It was there that he met Jill. Jill had recently moved to his town from Detroit. She was never fond of country music, but she quickly became fond of Rick.

Jill's dad was an avid car-racing fan, and from her earliest years she had gone to the races with him. When she worked up enough courage to invite Rick to go with her and her dad to a race, she was elated that he accepted. Though he had often watched car races on television Rick had never been to a race,

I had known Rick for a long time. One day shortly after he had been to the race with Jill and her dad, I saw him in the grocery store. He was eager to tell me about the race, but quickly added, "The most exciting thing about the race was being with Jill," he said. I saw the twinkle in his eye, and I knew that he had feelings for Jill.

Several months later they came in for premarital counseling. One of the first things they shared before we began our session was that the previous weekend they had been to the Grand Ole Opry. It seems that a group from the technical college had gotten together and decided this would be a good way to celebrate the end of the school year. Rick told me about the famous people he had seen, while Jill said, "The most exciting thing for me was being with Rick." Rick and Jill were demonstrating a fundamental principle. When an activity is to be a means of expressing love, the most important thing will not be the activity, but being with the other person. I was encouraged to see that they were willing to enter into each other's interests in order to have time together. I hoped that this expression of love would not stop when they got married.

Memories for Years to Come

One of the by-products of quality activities is that they provide a memory bank from which to draw in the years ahead. Fortunate is the couple who remembers an early morning stroll along the shoreline, the spring they planted the flower garden, the time they got poison ivy chasing the rabbit through the woods, the night they attended their first baseball game together, the one and only time they went skiing together and he broke his leg, the amusement parks, the concerts, the cathedrals, and, oh yes, the awe of standing beneath the waterfall after the two-mile hike. They can almost feel the mist as they remember. Those are memories of love, especially for the person whose primary love language is quality time and whose dialect is quality activities.

Whether it's a dating relationship or merely a friendship, such quality activities are not always easy to orchestrate. It will take careful planning. It may require you to give up some individual activities. It will mean you do some things that you don't particularly enjoy, but it will give you the pleasures of loving, entering into another's world, and learning to speak the love language of quality time.

THE FIVE LOVE LANGUAGES — SINGLES EDITION

THINGS TO THINK ABOUT

1. To what degree was the love language of quality time spoken by your parents to each other, and to you?

2. Are you energized when you spend quality time with others, or does it tend to deplete you emotionally?

3. With whom have you spent quality time this week? Was your time together primarily quality conversation or quality activities?

4. Would it be wise for you to give some quality time to one or both of your parents this week? This month? If so, why not put it on your schedule now?

5. In your circle of friends, who seems to be asking for quality time? Is this a relationship you would like to enhance? If so, why not set aside some quality time for them right now?

7

love language #5:
PHYSICAL TOUCH

WHEN WE WERE BABIES, before we could even crawl or eat solid food, we thrived on love. Numerous research projects in the area of child development have come to the same conclusion: Babies who are held, hugged, and touched tenderly develop a healthier emotional life than those who are left for long periods of time without physical contact. The same is true of the elderly. Visit some nursing homes and you will find that the residents who receive affirming touch have a more positive spirit and generally do better than those who are not touched. Tender, affirming physical touch is a fundamental language of love.

What is true for infants and the elderly is also true for single adults of all ages. One single young lady said, "It's funny that no one hesitates to touch a baby or pat a strange dog, but here I sit sometimes dying to have someone touch me and no one does." She was then apologetic for letting her needs be known. She concluded, "I guess that we don't trust letting people know the fact that we all like to be touched because we're afraid that people will misinterpret. So we sit back in loneliness and physical isolation."[1] It has been my observation that thousands of single adults can identify with this young lady's honest sentiments.

The body is made for touching. Of the five senses, touching, unlike the other four, is not limited to one localized area of the body. Tiny tactile receptors are located throughout the body. When those receptors are touched or pressed, nerves carry impulses to the brain, the brain interprets these impulses, and we perceive that the thing that touched us is warm or cold, hard or soft. It causes pain or pleasure. We may also interpret it as either a loving or hostile touch.

Some parts of the body are more sensitive than others. The tips of our fingers and the tip of our nose are highly sensitive. So is the tip of the tongue. In contrast, the back of the shoulders is the least sensitive area. The difference is due to the fact that the tiny tactile receptors are not scattered evenly over the body but are arranged in clusters. Our purpose, however, is not to understand the neurological basis of the sense of touch, but rather its psychological importance.

Physical touch can make or break a relationship. It can communicate hate or love. If the person's primary love language is physical touch, your touches will speak much louder than the words "I love you" or "I hate you." Withhold touches and you will isolate and raise doubts about your love. A tender hug communicates love to any child, but it shouts love to the child whose primary love language is physical touch. The same is true of single adults. When you listen to a friend who is feeling down and answer with a clasp of the shoulder, you declare loudly, "I love you. I care, and you are not alone."

When your body is touched, you are touched much more deeply than the mere physical contact. When someone withdraws from your body, they distance themselves from you emotionally. In our society shaking hands is a way of communicating openness and social closeness to another individual. When, on rare occasions, a man refuses to shake hands with another, it communicates a message that things are not right in their relationship.

ALL TOUCHES ARE NOT CREATED EQUAL

A touch of love may take many forms. Since touch receptors are located throughout the body, lovingly touching another individual almost anywhere can be an expression of love. Keep in mind that all touches are not created equal. Learn from the person whom you are touching what he or she perceives as a loving touch.

Appropriate and Inappropriate

There are appropriate and inappropriate ways to touch members of the opposite sex in every society. The recent attention to sexual harassment in Western culture has highlighted the danger of touching a member of the opposite sex in a way that is considered sexually inappropriate. This type of touch will not only fail to communicate love; it may result in much more serious problems as well.

Of course, physical abuse—inflicting bodily harm on another—is also inappropriate. Among single adults, the overall rate for severe violence is nearly five times as high for cohabiting couples when compared with married couples.[2] (We will discuss the nature of and right responses to physical abuse later in this chapter.)

Implicit and Explicit

Love touches may be implicit and subtle, requiring only a moment. Jen sometimes puts a hand on her mother's shoulder as she pours a cup of tea. Sometimes she pats her mom on the back as she turns to walk away. In contrast, explicit touches, such as a back rub or foot rub, demand your full attention. Such touches obviously take more time, not only in actual touching, but in developing your understanding of how to communicate love to another person. If a back massage communicates love loudly to someone you care about, then the time, money, and energy you spend in learning to be a good masseur or masseuse will be well invested.

Implicit love touches require little time but much thought, especially if physical touch is not your primary love language and if you did not grow up in a "touching family." As an adult, you can convey love to a parent or sibling simply yet powerfully. Sitting close to Mom or Dad on the couch as you watch your favorite television program together may communicate your love loudly. Touching a family member as you walk through the room where he or she is sitting takes only a moment.

SENSITIVE TOUCHES

Almost instinctively in a time of crisis we hug one another. Why? Because physical touch is a powerful communicator of love. In a time of crisis, more than anything we need to feel loved. We can't always change events, but we can survive if we feel loved.

Single adults are not exempt from the normal crises of life. The death of parents is inevitable. Automobile accidents cripple and kill thousands each year. Disease is no respecter of persons. Disappointments are a part of life. The most important thing you can do for a friend in a time of crisis is to love him or her. If her primary love language is physical touch, nothing is more important than holding her as she cries. Your words may mean little, but your physical touch will communicate that you care. Crises provide a unique opportunity for expressing love. Your tender touches will be remembered long after the crisis has passed. Your failure to touch may also never be forgotten.

How many successful single adults would give up their kingdom to have a genuine, tender hug from their dad? A pat on the back, a kiss on the cheek, a tender touch to the arm, holding hands, and embracing are all dialects of the love language physical touch. Julia revealed her own primary love language when she said, "One of the things I like most about my church is that the people are huggers. When I leave church, my love tank is full. I can make it through a difficult week knowing that the people at my church love me."

On the other hand, some single adults may not respond positively to physical touch. If, when you give a work associate a pat on the back he stiffens up and withdraws, he is communicating that physical touch is not his primary love language. However, another person in the same office might feel affirmed by your pat on the back. The purpose of love is to enhance the well-being of another, not to satisfy your own desires. Therefore, learning to speak another person's primary love language is the most effective way of loving others.

PHYSICAL TOUCH AND SEXUALITY

We cannot discuss physical touch as an emotional love language without also discussing how this affects human sexuality. Nor can we discuss physical touch without recognizing how twenty-first-century sexual mores influence our ways of touching. Today's single adult lives in the cultural aftermath of the sexual revolution that began half a century ago.

Freud and the Sexual Revolution

This revolution found its roots in the early 1900s' writings of Sigmund Freud, the father of psychoanalysis. Freud emphasized the effect of sex on behavior. According to Freud, the full and uninhibited satisfaction of all instinctual desires would create mental health and happiness. Freud's concept of sexuality, though widely accepted, has not been validated by research in the past fifty years.

One decade before the 1960s' sexual revolution exploded, Erich Fromm, a student of Freud, chose to oppose his teacher. In his classic work *The Art of Loving*, Fromm wrote, "The obvious clinical facts demonstrate that men — and women — who devote their lives to unrestricted sexual satisfaction do not attain happiness, and very often suffer from severe neurotic conflicts or symptoms. The complete satisfaction of all instinctual needs is not only not a basis for happiness, it does not even guarantee sanity."[3]

Pitirim Sorokin, a leading sociologist of his day, predicted that if Freud's ideas were applied to society it would destroy the meaning of human sexuality:

> *The sex-obsessed society unhesitatingly breaks both divine and human law, and blows to smithereens all values. Like a tornado, it leaves in its path a legion of corpses, a multitude of wrecked lives, an untold amount of suffering, and ugly debris of broken standards. It destroys the real freedom of normal love; and in lieu of enriching and ennobling the sexual passion, it reduces it to mere copulation.*[4]

The Outcome of the Revolution

The last forty years of research have overwhelmingly documented the accuracy of Sorokin's sociological prophecy. Singles and married people are acquiring sexually transmitted diseases in unprecedented numbers. Glenn Stanton, a social research analyst, says, "With the great divorce between marriage and sexuality, the dream of a fulfilling sex life is more elusive to more people than it has been at any time in our nation's history." His conclusion is that "sex does not need to be liberated, rather it simply needs to be confined to its proper and most productive domain. Decades of research show that this place is lifelong, monogamous marriage."[5]

The commonly held idea that cohabitation will lead to a healthier marriage has been shattered by numerous research projects. These studies, conducted in several Western countries, including Canada, Sweden, New Zealand, and the United States, have found that those who cohabit before marriage have substantially higher divorce rates than those who do not. In fact, the rates range from 50 to 100 percent higher.[6]

Prof. Jan Stets of Washington State University, one of the most noted researchers on the issue of cohabitation, concluded, "Cohabiting couples compared to married couples have less healthy relationships. They have lower relationship quality, lower stability, and a higher level of disagreements."[7]

The Quest for Meaning in Sex

The popular idea is that sex is a biological need on the same level as thirst. If you are thirsty, drink water. If you are hungry, eat food. If you have sexual desire, fulfill it. Professor Sorokin's prophecy has come true: Sex has been reduced to mere copulation. But the fact is none of us really believe that. We may drink water and eat food at any restaurant in the country, but having sex whenever, wherever, and with whomever does not meet the deep longing of the human soul for an exclusive sexual relationship.

A major national sex survey from the University of Chicago found that 95 percent of cohabiters and 99 percent of married people expected their partner to be sexually faithful to them.[8] Something deep within us says, "Sex is intimate and should be shared with someone to whom I have a deep commitment."

When our sexual relationship is not exclusive, we feel violated. The

THE FIVE LOVE LANGUAGES — SINGLES EDITION

reality is that married men are far more likely to be faithful to their wives than are cohabiting men with their domestic partners. Research indicates that the cohabiting male is four times more likely to be unfaithful as the married man, and the cohabiting woman is eight times more likely to be unfaithful to her "lover" as a married woman.[9]

There is a reason why Christianity and most major world religions have a high regard for human sexuality, viewing it not as a biological drive on the level with thirst, but as a gift from God to be fully and freely expressed between a man and woman who are committed to each other by the covenant of marriage. All the sociological, anthropological, and psychological research of the past fifty years has validated this view of human sexuality.

The single adult in contemporary society must make the choice between Freud and the facts: uninhibited sexual expression or reserving sexual intercourse for the one to whom you are willing to make a lifelong commitment. This is no minor choice. It affects your physical and emotional health, as well as sexual satisfaction, for years to come.

APPROPRIATE TOUCHES—SAME SEX AND OPPOSITE SEX

Having made this important and necessary digression from our discussion of the love language physical touch, let me return now to say that there are many appropriate loving, affirming dialects in which one can express the love language of physical touch to members of the opposite sex. These may occur in a dating relationship, a friendship, or among coworkers.

The love language of physical touch may also be spoken to members of the same sex. Such expressions have nothing to do with homosexuality, but are expressions of sincere love and appreciation for a friend, a roommate, or someone you interact with in a business or social context.

The emphasis of this chapter and of this love language has little to do with sexuality, but everything to do with expressing emotional love to others by means of affirming physical touch.

Learn to Touch

However, for some single adults, giving and receiving love via physical touch will not be easy. Their lives have been scarred by physical or sexual abuse when they were children or teenagers. For these individuals, Christian counseling offers the most effective means of healing the memories of past abuse. Without such inner healing, it will be very difficult for most people to form healthy, long-term relationships.

Other singles have not been traumatized by physical and sexual abuse but simply grew up in families that were not "touching" families. Thus, the whole idea of physical touch seems to them an invasion of personal space and is emotionally uncomfortable. For these singles, it is simply a matter of learning to speak a new love language.

"I'm Not a 'Touchy-Feely' Person"

Marti, a twenty-four-year-old never-married single, said to me, "I'm just not a 'touchy-feely' person. I don't necessarily enjoy people hugging me, and I certainly don't initiate hugs to others. I guess it was the way I was brought up. In my family, we loved each other, but we didn't do much touching.

"The problem is I'm dating a guy that I really like, but he's complaining because I don't seem to be interested in kissing and hugging. I don't mind kissing if I'm really passionate, but hugging every time I see him or holding hands in public just doesn't seem natural to me."

I knew that Marti had a sharp learning curve to face, but I hoped that her desire to continue this relationship might stimulate her to learn to speak the love language of physical touch. After I explained the five love languages and that each person has a primary love language, Marti exclaimed, "Well, my primary love language certainly is not physical touch!"

"What is your primary love language?" I inquired.

"I think it's words of affirmation," she said. "I really feel good when John tells me how pretty I am or makes some comment about something I'm wearing. Maybe that's why I'm hurt so deeply when he complains about my failing to take initiative in hugging and kissing. It seemed to me like he was putting too much emphasis on touching. It was as if that's all that mattered to him. But maybe physical touch is his primary love language."

I could tell that Marti was going to be a fast learner, so I said, "If physical touch is John's primary love language, would you like to learn to speak it?"

"Yes," she said, "but I'm not sure I can ever be a 'touchy-feely' person."

"You don't have to change who you are," I said. "But you can learn to speak any of the five love languages, and you can certainly learn to speak the language of physical touch."

"How do I do that?"

"By trying. Languages are learned one word at a time, or in this case, one touch at a time. Why don't you begin by hugging your parents the next time you see them?" I suggested.

"You mean, just walk up and hug them?" she asked.

"Yes. Do you think you can do that?"

"I guess so," she said, "but I don't know how they will respond."

"Learn by Doing"

"That really doesn't matter," I said. "You are trying to learn to speak the language of physical touch, and you learn by doing. In fact, I am going to suggest that every time you see your parents for the next two months, hug them when you arrive and hug them when you leave. We know that the hugging will not hurt them, and it will certainly help you begin to feel a little more comfortable speaking the love language of physical touch.

"Then you can begin to turn your attention to John. Taking his hand as you leave the car and walk toward the mall may be difficult the first time you do it, but it will come easier the second time. At the end of the evening, initiate a hug and at least a kiss on the cheek. The more often you do this, the more comfortable it will feel."

Marti seemed a little hesitant, but she said, "Okay, I'll try it and see what happens."

It was a brief conversation, but I hoped that Marti's strong motivation to enhance her relationship with John would give her encouragement to try what I had suggested.

The next time I saw Marti, she said, "It's working. It's even helping my relationship with my parents. The first time I hugged my mother, it was like hugging a flagpole. Now she is hugging me back."

"How's your relationship with John?" I asked.

"It's going great. I think John really appreciates my taking the initiative in holding hands, hugging, and kissing. And it's beginning to feel more comfortable for me. John is a great guy."

"I assume he is giving you words of affirmation," I said.

"Oh, yes, and no more complaints," said Marti.

The good news about the five love languages is that all of them can be learned. Thus, you can deepen all your relationships by learning and speaking a person's primary love language. Becoming fluent in the love language of physical touch also requires that you be sensitive to the desires of the other person. The *time*, *place*, and *manner* in which you touch are all important.

TIMING IS EVERYTHING

Timing is largely determined by the mood and desire of the other person. A single mom said, "I can tell when my son wants to be touched by the way he closes the door when he enters the house. If he slams the door, it's a 'don't touch me' mood. If he takes time to quietly close the door, he is saying, 'I'm open to a touch, Mom.'" Another single mom said, "I can tell when my daughter doesn't want to be touched by the distance she stands from me when she talks. If she stands on the other side of the room while talking, I know that she doesn't want to be touched, but if she comes up and stands close to me, I know she is open to a loving touch."

Often people communicate their mood by their body language — how close they are to you, or whether their arms are folded, for example. Observing body language will tell you the appropriate time for touching others. It is almost always inappropriate to touch someone when he or she is angry. Anger is an emotion that pushes people away from each other. If you attempt to hug a person when he or she is angry, you will most likely be rebuffed. Here is where physical touch can come across as an effort to control; it strikes at the person's need for independence. And he will pull away from your touch.

Touches are usually appropriate after a person has accomplished something great. It is a means of celebrating victory. This is often observed on the athletic field, but it works just as well in the office or in a dating relationship. Conversely, times of failure are also times for expressing the love language of physical touch. When people are down on themselves because they have not lived up to their potential, physical touch can communicate genuine love and concern.

THE APPROPRIATE SETTING

Knowing the proper situation for touching is also important. This is a matter of setting, not sexuality. The ten-year-old welcomed his mother's embrace after each little league football game was over. He rushed to wherever his mother was standing and waited for her positive words and affirming touch. But at sixteen when the varsity game is over, he will not be looking for his mom, and he hopes she will not be looking for him. Single moms and dads will look for appropriate settings to affirm their children and teenagers through this love language.

The same is true in dating relationships. Hugging and kissing when the two of you are alone is very different from hugging and kissing in a crowded mall. What is appropriate in one place may not be appropriate in another. The key is to respect the desires of the person you are dating. To force physical touch in places where they are not comfortable is not an expression of love but of selfishness. Which brings us to the manner in which physical touch is expressed.

HOW YOU GO ABOUT IT

Here we are talking about not only the kinds of touches we give but the manner in which we give them. There are numerous ways in which to express affection by physical touch. Hugs, kisses, back rubs, pats, tender touches, massages, and even arm wrestling are all appropriate ways to speak the love language of physical touch. However, the process is not as simple as it sounds. Not everyone likes the same kinds of touches. Some people like a hand on their shoulder and others don't. Every individual is unique. If you want to be successful in relationships, you must learn not only the love language, but also the dialect in which the other person best receives love.

If the person you are dating doesn't enjoy shoulder rubs, it would be a mistake to force such touch upon him/her simply because you like shoulder rubs. We must not force our own love language on another person; rather we must learn to speak his/her love language. If the person you are dating says, "I don't like that" in response to your efforts to physically touch him/her, then back off and find another method of physical touch. To insist on continuing is to communicate the opposite of love. It is saying that you are not sensitive to their needs.

Don't make the mistake of believing that what you like is what everyone else around you likes too. The whole concept of the five love languages is learning to speak the other's language, not just perfecting your own. What makes the other person feel loved is the key question. If physical touch is her primary love language, then you must find the particular kinds of touch that communicate love to her. It'd be a lot easier to love, though a whole lot more boring, if everyone felt loved in the same way. The process of loving is complicated by the other person's own preferences.

Obviously, the emotional climate in which you give physical touch is extremely important. If you slap a person on the shoulder because you are frustrated with his behavior, he will not feel loved. However, the same touch in a different context may be a genuine expression of love.

INAPPROPRIATE PHYSICAL TOUCH

I wish I didn't have to write the next few paragraphs. I wish the terms *physical abuse* and *sexual abuse* were not so common in our society. But the reality is that a significant number of singles do experience abuse in dating relationships, particularly in cohabiting relationships. We see the more dramatic examples on the evening news, but many people suffer silently, and sometimes their closest friends and family are not even aware of the abuse.

Physical Abuse

In *The Five Love Languages of Teenagers*, I defined physical abuse this way:

> *Physical abuse is causing physical harm by beating, hitting, kicking, and so forth out of anger rather than play. The key word is anger. Some [singles] have never learned to handle anger in a constructive manner. When they are angered by someone's behavior, the flow of vicious words is followed by physical violence. Slaps, pushes, shoves, choking, holding, shaking, and hitting are all abusive behaviors. . . . Where this occurs, we can be certain that [love is not being expressed.] Positive words and expressions of physical affection which follow such angry outbursts will always appear hollow. . . . The [human] heart does not easily recover from such physical abuse.*[10]

A sincere and honest apology is not enough. The individual who is abusing must seek help in breaking these destructive patterns and learning positive anger management skills. Explosive anger will not simply go away with the passing of time. If you are dating someone who is physically abusive, I would encourage you to break off the relationship and insist that the person get counseling for his (or her) behavior. If you are not emotionally strong enough to do this, then I would encourage you to go for personal counseling and gain the emotional strength and knowledge necessary so that you can take constructive steps to protect yourself from such abuse. You are not serving the cause of love when you allow abusive behavior to continue.

Sexual Abuse

Sexual abuse is taking advantage of a relationship to obtain sexual favors in order to satisfy one's own sexual desires. When one person is forced to perform sexual acts that they do not desire to perform, they are being sexually abused. Sexual abuse can also occur in other settings as well (not just a dating relationship); sometimes it occurs in the context of drug abuse or another addictive behavior.

Some single adults are so desperate for emotional love that they allow themselves to be treated as sexual objects rather than persons. Again, I would encourage such singles to seek individual counseling to gain the emotional energy and self-respect to stop abusive behavior. Any forced sexual behavior is the opposite of love. It is nothing more than self-gratification.

Sexual abuse over a period of time breeds bitterness, hatred, and often depression. Sometimes such emotions erupt in violent behavior.

The first step is to acknowledge this behavior as being wrong. The second step is to seek professional counseling, share the problem, and begin the process of healing. Yes, such a bold step will be costly, may bring embarrassment, may disrupt your dating relationship, and may create emotional stress for you. But failure to do so will be more costly in the long run.

The love language of physical touch never uses force but always seeks the appropriate time, place, and manner in which to express affirming touch. Physical touch is one of the fundamental languages of love, and it is well worth the time, energy, and effort it takes to learn to speak this language effectively.

Portions of this chapter have been adapted from The Five Love Languages, *chapter 7.*

THINGS TO THINK ABOUT

1. What types of physical touch do you consider affirming?

2. What kinds of touches make you feel uncomfortable?

3. To what degree did your parents speak the love language of physical touch to you? To each other?

4. In your circle of friends, who are the "touchers"? People whose primary love language is *Physical Touch* usually like to be touched. In what way might you reciprocate their love?

5. Looking back over today or yesterday, what types of physical touches did you give to others? How did they seem to respond?

6. If touching comes easy for you, whom have you encountered who seemed to draw back from touching? Why do you think this is true?

8

you go first:

DISCOVER YOUR PRIMARY
LOVE LANGUAGE

ANIMALS DON'T SIT AROUND campfires and spin tales of past experiences, present difficulties, and future desires. But people do. One of the things that sets man apart from animals is his ability to communicate by means of words. Language is distinctively human.

Another element of languages is that they are extremely diverse. I remember sitting in a linguistics lab trying to phonetically record the sounds of a language I had never heard. Even when I recorded sounds, they made no sense to me at all. They communicated nothing to me because I didn't understand the meaning behind the words.

We all grow up learning to speak the language of our culture. If you grew up in a multicultural setting, you may be able to speak several languages. However, the language you learned to speak first, usually the language of your parents, will be your primary or native language. It has sometimes been called the "heart language." Your native language is the one you understand best and the one that communicates to you most clearly. You may speak a second language or even a third very fluently, but you will always be partial to your native tongue.

The same is true when we talk about the languages of love. Out of the five fundamental languages, each of us has a primary love language. It is the one that speaks most deeply to us emotionally. Having heard the five love languages — words of affirmation, gifts, acts of service, quality time, and physical touch — some singles will immediately recognize their own primary love language. Others, because they have never thought of love in this paradigm, will be uncertain of their primary love language.

WHICH ONE IS YOURS?

Two categories of people typically struggle to discover their primary love language. The first consists of singles who have always felt loved and who received all five love languages from their parents. They speak all five rather fluently, but they're not sure which one speaks most deeply to them. The other category is composed of singles who have never felt loved. They grew up in very dysfunctional families and were never secure in the love of parents or other significant adults in their lives. They don't know which language would make them feel loved because they are not really sure what it means to feel loved. This chapter is designed to help those people who are not certain of their primary love language. But also keep in mind that the following pages ought to be helpful for everyone else to hone their own language skills as well.

1. Observe Your Own Behavior

So how do you discover your primary love language? Probably it would be best to start by asking yourself, *How do I most typically express love and appreciation to other people*? If you regularly hear yourself encouraging other people by giving words of affirmation, then perhaps that is your primary love language. You are doing for others what you wish they would do for you. If you are a back-patter, hand-shaker, or arm-toucher, then perhaps your love language is physical touch. If you are constantly giving gifts to others on special occasions and for no occasion at all, then gifts may be your primary love language. If you are the initiator in setting up lunch appointments or inviting people over to your house for the evening, then quality time may be your love language. If you are the kind of person who doesn't wait until someone asks but observes what needs to be done and pitches in and does it, then acts of service is likely your primary love language.

Please notice that I am using the words *perhaps, may be,* and *likely.* The reason I am being tentative is because my research has indicated that about 25 percent of adults typically speak one love language but wish to receive another language. On the other hand, for about 75 percent of us, the language we speak most often is the language we desire. We love others in the manner in which we would like to be loved.

2. Observe What You Request of Others

If you regularly ask friends to help you with projects, then acts of service may be your love language. If you find yourself saying to friends who are going on a trip, "Be sure and bring me something," then your love language is probably receiving gifts. If you ask a close friend to give you a back rub, or you express rather freely, "Could you give me a hug?" then physical touch is likely your primary love language. If you are regularly asking friends to go shopping with you, to take a trip together, or to come over to your house for dinner, you are asking for quality time. If you hear yourself asking, "Does this look all right? Did I do the report the way you wanted it? Do you think I did the right thing?" you are asking for words of affirmation.

Our requests tend to indicate our emotional needs. Therefore, observing what you request of others may clearly reveal your primary love language.

3. Listen to Your Complaints

The things about which you complain (whether expressed verbally or only in your head) can be very telling in figuring out your primary love language.

Brad was about six months into his first job after college when I asked him, "How are things going?"

"Okay, I guess. It seems like nobody really appreciates what I do and that what I do is never enough."

Knowing that he was familiar with the five love languages, I said, "Your primary love language is words of affirmation, right?"

He nodded his head while he said, "Yes, and I guess that's why I'm not really all that happy with my job." Brad's complaint clearly revealed his primary love language.

If you complain that your friends no longer have time for you, your love language is likely quality time. If you complain that only one friend gave you a birthday present, your language is likely gifts. If you complain about not having a good hug in the last two months, physical touch is probably your language. If your complaint is that no one ever helps you and they expect you to do everything, then acts of service is probably your love language.

Our complaints reveal our deep emotional hurts. The opposite of what hurts you most is probably your love language. If you received love in that language, the hurt would go away and you would feel appreciated.

4. Ask the Right Questions

If you are currently in a dating relationship, you've got a great opportunity to discover your primary love language. Ask and answer the following questions: "What do I like most about the person I'm dating? What does he or she do or say that makes me desire to be with him/her?" Your answers will be very enlightening.

Another approach would be to ask yourself: "What would be an ideal spouse to me? If I could have the perfect mate, what would she/he be like?" Your picture of a perfect mate should give you some idea of your primary love language.

If you are not currently in a romantic relationship, you may ask: "What do I want most in a friendship?" Complete the following sentence: "An ideal friend would _____." Your answer will probably reveal your primary love language.

5. The Love Language Profile

You may also wish to use the love language profile that appears in the appendix of this book. This profile asks you to make choices between two options and to record your response in the appropriate column. The results will help you figure out your love language.

WHICH LOVE LANGUAGE IS THEIRS?

Discovering your own love language helps you understand why you feel more loved and appreciated by certain people than you do others. But what about the other side of the coin? There is certainly satisfaction in receiving love, but there is also much satisfaction in giving love (maybe even more). If you are to be an effective lover, you must learn how to discover other people's primary love languages.

So how can you figure this out? You can't simply walk up and say,

"What's your primary love language?" unless, of course, they have read the book and want to discuss it. Let's assume that you would like to discover the love language of your parents, siblings, coworkers, friends, or someone with whom you have a romantic relationship.

Observe Their Expressions, Complaints, and Requests

Let's begin with the obvious. You could take the approaches suggested in the first half of this chapter in discovering your own primary love language. That would involve observing how they express love to other people. If you observe your father expressing acts of service to your mother and other people, then acts of service may be his primary love language. On the other hand, if he welcomes you with a hug every time you go home, then his love language is likely physical touch. If your coworker typically gives words of affirmation and appreciation to others, then that is probably his/her love language. For many people, this isn't a hard code to crack. For others, who are not as free in their expressions of love, you may have more difficulty catching them expressing love.

Therefore, you might ask yourself, "What do they complain about most often?" If your roommate periodically says things like, "I need a little more help around here," or "I'm getting tired of picking up your wet towel," his love language may be acts of service. If your boyfriend says with a bit of frustration, "You don't ever initiate a kiss. Just a peck on the cheek would be a good starting place," he is revealing that physical touch is his primary love language. If your girlfriend says, "Frankly, I'm upset that you didn't send me flowers or anything on my birthday," and your response is, "I took you out to dinner. Doesn't that count?" she may respond, "Yes, and I appreciate that. But I wanted something to remind me of the day." She is revealing the importance of gifts.

The third approach would be to notice what they request most often.

The mother who asks, "Could you come over for dinner this Sunday?" is asking for quality time. The coworker who says, "When you go to the conference, could you pick up some 'freebies' for me?" is requesting gifts. The friend who says, "Could we take a walk?" is asking for quality time.

None of this is terribly difficult or painful—it just takes an observant mindset and a desire to love others effectively. Observing their behavior and listening to their complaints and requests may well show you the primary love language of others.

Margo's Discovery: Don't Be Afraid to Ask Questions

There are other ways to discover a person's primary love language. One of the most compelling ways is to ask questions. If you wish to know what is going on inside the mind of someone else, then ask questions. The questions must be well chosen and must be expressions of genuine desire for information.

For example, Margo said to her mother, "Mom, I've been thinking about it, and this year on my birthday, I would like to do something special for you to express my appreciation to you for giving me life. I want you to think about it, and next week I want you to tell me what you would like for me to do."

"Honey, you don't need to do anything for me. I know you appreciate me."

"Well, I hope so, thanks for saying that," said Margo, "but I want to do something special for you, so think about it."

The next week when Margo dropped by to see her mother, she found her working in the flowers. Her mother finished what she was doing, washed her hands with the hose, and said, "I've got some fresh lemonade inside." As they walked into the house, Margo commented on how beautiful her mother's garden was.

"It's rained a lot this summer," her mother said.

As they drank their lemonade, Margo asked her mother, "Have you thought about what I asked you last week about my birthday?"

"Yes, I've thought about it," her mother said.

"Well, what would you like me to do?" Margo was not prepared for what her mother said.

"This may be asking too much, but if you really want to do something that would make me happy, I would like for us to spend an entire day together, from early in the morning to late at night. We can go shopping. We can take a walk in the park like we used to when you were a little girl. We can go out to have lunch, or we can just sit around the house all day. I don't care what we do. I'd just like to spend a whole day with you again like we did when you were growing up. It doesn't have to be on your birthday. It can be before or after."

Margo responded with a question mark in her voice. "Well, Mom, I'd be glad to do that. But are you sure that's really what you want?"

"I'm sure," her mother said. "I can't think of anything I would enjoy more than spending a day with you."

If Margo's intent was to figure out her mother's primary love language, she has made her discovery. Loudly and clearly her mother has spoken, "Quality time is my love language." And she learned simply by asking her mother what gift she'd like most.

Later, Margo reflected on their conversation. She realized that since she had moved back to town after graduating from college, she had spent only snippets of time with her mother. She checked in almost every week, but normally it was only a fifteen- to thirty-minute visit. After thinking about it some more, she remembered her mother's comments from time to time, "Can't you stay a little longer?" Remembering these words confirmed to her that quality time was her mother's primary love language.

Helen's Discovery: Good Gifts are Different for Everyone

At age fifty-six, Helen unexpectedly became a single adult again. Only nine months earlier her husband had been killed in a car accident. In an attempt to get her out of the house, a friend invited her to an adult singles meeting where I was speaking.

"I didn't really want to come to this meeting," she later told me. "I don't feel like a single adult. I feel like I'm still married. It's just that my husband is no longer here. But, I'm glad I came," she said. "I've never heard about love languages. I think I need to apply this in my relationship with my son."

Helen had one son, Brett, who was now thirty-two. He had married right out of college and divorced two years later. Since then, he lived alone and only sporadically made contact with his parents. However, since the death of his dad, he came around more often, and Helen was hoping they could have a closer relationship. "I think I need to discover his love language," Helen said. I suggested she give Brett a chance to show his love language by responding to the following statement: "Since your dad has died, we're the only two left. You have been so helpful to me these last few months, I'd like to do something to show you how much I appreciate what you have done. What can I do?"

Later, I got a letter from Helen: "I have now discovered Brett's love language. It is clearly acts of service." His response to his mom's initial inquiry was "Mom, the greatest thing you could do for me would be to sew some buttons back on my shirts. I must have a dozen shirts that are missing buttons. I know you've got a drawer full of buttons in there. Maybe you could find some that would match and make the shirts functional again."

"A dozen turned out to be fifteen," said Helen, "and I've also sewn buttons on six trousers and four coats. Recently, he asked me if I would like to come over and show him how to get stains out of his carpet. I feel like he's letting me back into his life again. I don't want to be too aggressive, so I'm only responding to specific requests that he makes. But I can tell he's appreciative of what I'm doing. I feel like I'm speaking his love language."

Experiment a Little Bit

Another way to go about discovering someone's primary love language is to try a few different things and see what works. Since you don't know the person's primary language, and perhaps are not close enough to formulate a sincere question, you simply focus a period of time expressing one of the five love languages and observe how the person responds. For example, you might take a week and focus on positive words, making it your goal to speak at least one affirming word to the person each day. The next week you give the person one or two small tokens of appreciation as gifts. It could be a five-dollar Starbucks gift card or a funny card you picked out with her in mind.

The following week you try to have at least one extended conversation with the person — speaking the love language of quality time. Then the next week you focus on finding something you could do for the individual, hopefully something you have heard her mention that she would like someone to do for her. The last week you give her affirming, appropriate touches ("appropriate" would obviously depend upon the nature of the relationship).

The week you are speaking the person's primary love language you will observe a difference in his or her response to you. Their eyes will light up, they'll seem to be more appreciative than normal, and they may even write you a note expressing appreciation for what you have said or done.

It takes time, effort, and thought to discover another person's primary love language. But if you want to be effective in communicating love and appreciation, then it is time well invested. Learning to speak another person's primary love language is the key to communicating to them on an emotional level that you care about their well-being. In the next chapter we will discuss how this information can enhance family relationships.

THINGS TO THINK ABOUT

1. If you know your primary love language, how did you discover it? If you do not know your love language by now, take the love language profile found at the conclusion of the book.

2. Do you know the primary love language of your dad... mom... brother... sister? If not, which approach do you think would be the best way to make this discovery?

3. Who are your two closest friends? Do you know their primary love language? If not, answer the following questions:

   a. *How does he/she most often express love and appreciation to others?*

   b. *What do they request of you most often?*

   c. *What have they complained about recently?*

   If the answers to these questions do not reveal their love language, then perhaps you could take the following approach: "I really value our friendship, and I want you to think about us and then tell me one thing I could do that would enhance our relationship."

4. Make a list of the significant people in your life. If you know their primary love language, write it beside their name. If not, then using the ideas in this chapter, plan your strategy to discover it.

9

family:

CONNECT THE DOTS WITH YOUR IMMEDIATE FAMILY

I MET SUSAN ABOARD the *MSS Amsterdam*, cruising the Inside Passage of Alaska. The night before I had given a lecture on the five love languages. "I've been thinking about what you said last night," she said. "It has opened my eyes about my relationship with my dad.

"About a year ago my mom died, and I moved to Chicago to help my dad, but it's been a very difficult year. He is always asking me to do things for him, things that he could do for himself. I have felt like he was trying to manipulate me and control my life. Now I know that his love language is acts of service. He has been asking me for love.

"When I was getting ready to paint my house, he said, 'I'll come down and hold the ladder for you.' I didn't want that. It takes twice as long with him there. I know now that he was expressing love to me using the language he knew best. This has given me a whole new perspective about my dad."

Susan had made a significant insight into the secret of family connections. Love *should* begin at home with husbands and wives loving each other and with parents loving children. In this ideal context, children learn to receive and give love freely. However, many people grew up in less than ideal homes. Many parents have never learned how to speak each other's primary love language; nor have they learned to speak the love languages of their children. Consequently, many singles grew up in a home where they knew intellectually that their parents loved them, but they did not always feel loved. In the teenage years, relationships with parents became strained, and now that they are adults, they have no close bond with their parents.

The purpose of this chapter is to help you enhance relationships with your parents and siblings. You may have a strong, positive relationship with your parents and siblings, or you may be struggling, even estranged from your immediate family. No matter where you're starting from, understanding and applying the principles you have read in the first eight chapters of this book can greatly enhance family relationships.

LOVING OUR PARENTS

Enhancing or reestablishing a relationship with a parent may have a profound impact upon a person's emotional well-being. It isn't random chance that one of the ten fundamental commandments given to ancient Israel was "Honor your father and your mother, so that you may live long in the land the Lord your God is giving you."[1] This benefit of developing a positive, loving relationship with one's parents is affirmed in the New Testament: "Honor your father and mother—which is the first commandment with a promise—that it may go well with you and that you may enjoy long life on the earth."[2]

Ideally, love should flow from parent to child. When this takes place and the child genuinely feels loved, it is easy for them to honor their parents. However, when a single adult grew up in a home where he felt unloved, abandoned, or abused, it is much more difficult to honor these parents. I believe that as adults we must take responsibility for enhancing the relationship with our parents; this is especially important if they were deficient in meeting our needs. There is nothing more important than love in this process. Love breaks down barriers, leaps over walls, and seeks the well-being of another.

The amazing thing about love is that it is not held captive by our emotions. We may feel hurt by our parents. We may feel abandoned, disappointed, frustrated, and even depressed, but we can still express love to them. Love is not an island of emotion, but rather an attitude that corresponds with appropriate behaviors. Love is the attitude that says, "I choose to look out for your interest. How may I serve you?" Then love responds with meaningful, positive behavior.

LOVE STIMULATES A RESPONSE

Such love does stimulate positive emotions. So we say, "I feel loved by that person," which means we have a deep emotional sense that they really care about us. It is this sense of being cared for that brings deep satisfaction to the human soul. When we feel loved, the natural response is to honor the person who is loving us, to hold him in high esteem. When there is mutual love and honor between parents and adult children, both experience a positive state of emotional health, which in turn positively affects their physical health, which results in longer, more fulfilling life.

No parental relationship is hopeless. As long as there is life, there is the potential for healing the past and carving a better relationship in the future. If your relationship with your parents is less than ideal, nothing holds more potential than your taking the initiative to learn their primary love languages and begin speaking them regularly. Because they are human, they desperately crave love. When you start proactively loving them in their language, they begin to feel your love and often reciprocate.

Therefore, you can take the initiative to love your parents in spite of your negative feelings. If and when your parents reciprocate your expressions of love using your love language, your negative feelings will dissipate and you will begin to feel loved by them. Of course reciprocated love is not guaranteed. But it often happens even in the most difficult and scarred relationships.

JENNIFER'S STORY
Looking for Her Birth Mother

Jennifer, thirty-four, is a never-married single who learned to speak the love languages of her adoptive parents, George and Martha, and her birth mother, Christina—but only after experiencing conflict with all three. The result is an extremely positive and close relationship with her adoptive parents and a loving relationship with her birth mother.

For the first thirteen years of Jennifer's life, George and Martha provided her with a stable and loving environment. However, when Jennifer turned fourteen, she began to express a desire to find and meet her birth mother. Her adoptive parents strongly opposed this idea. They knew that Jennifer's mother had been on drugs at the time of her birth and had had multiple sexual partners. They had no reason to believe that she was the kind of person who would have a positive impact on Jennifer's life.

Jennifer's reasoning at fourteen had been, "I want to meet my mother. If I don't like her, then fine, we don't have to have a relationship. But I want to meet her." George and Martha resisted Jennifer's pleas, because they genuinely thought it would not be good for her. The next two years were marked by frequent struggles over this and other matters. By age sixteen Jennifer felt deeply unloved by her adoptive parents and began taking the initiative to find her birth mother. With the help of a friend at school, Jennifer was able to locate her mother and give her a call. Her mother was elated to hear from her, and they arranged to get together.

They had lunch on several occasions and were relating to each other positively (all of this unknown to Jennifer's adoptive parents). Christina eventually invited Jennifer to her apartment to meet her live-in boyfriend. He was nice to Jennifer, and she liked him.

The Argument and the Lecture

After almost a year, George and Martha discovered what was going on and responded harshly.

"I can't believe you have done this to us," Martha said, "after all we have done for you."

"My mother is not a bad woman, and she loves me," said Jennifer.

"Then if she loves you so much, why don't you go live with her?" Martha could not believe what she had just said. "I don't mean that," she quickly added. "You don't need to live with her. She can't be good for you." Martha began to cry uncontrollably, and Jennifer walked out of the room.

That night she got a long lecture from her father about how they wanted only what was best for her and had loved her all these years and still loved her. He told Jennifer about her mother's drug problem and the lifestyle she had lived. "That is why we didn't want you to have contact with her," he said.

Jennifer listened. Her only response was, "I know you love me, Dad, but I want to have a relationship with my mother. I don't want to hurt you, but I can't just walk away from her now." George left the room, and Jennifer cried.

Her last year in high school was a troubled one, as Jennifer tried to maintain sporadic contact with Christina without discussing it with her parents. Then she went off to college where life became a lot easier. She was able to have contact with both her parents and her mother. If her parents raised questions about seeing her mother, she simply denied it, and her mother never asked about her adoptive parents. She was just happy to have Jennifer in her life.

At the beginning of Jennifer's junior year in college, her mother's boyfriend moved out, and her mother sank into a deep depression. During this time Christina returned to drugs and a year later ended up in a rehabilitation center. Jennifer had little contact with her during that year except an occasional phone call that she initiated and which usually left her in tears. Jennifer began suffering through some depression and went for counseling. During those counseling sessions she was able to work through her feelings of abandonment by her mother and being controlled by her parents.

Learning a Few New Languages

She came to recognize that her birth mother had made the wisest decision possible at that time in her life and that her adoptive parents were sincerely thinking about her best interests when they tried to keep her from making contact with her mother. She intellectually understood what had happened, but she still struggled with feelings of abandonment. "I'm not sure anybody really loves me," she told her counselor. "Intellectually I know my mother loves me, and I know my parents love me. But emotionally a lot of the time I don't feel loved by anyone."

During that session her therapist gave her a copy of *The Five Love Languages*. "This book was originally written for married couples, helping them learn how to love each other," the counselor said, "but I want you to read it, because I think it will help you understand the dynamics of love."

Jennifer read the book and spent several sessions discussing it with her counselor. She came to realize that her own primary love language was words of affirmation. That's why she was so attracted to her mother when she made initial contact. Her mother gave her so many affirming words. Conversely, that's why she began to feel unloved by her parents when they opposed the idea of their fourteen-year-old daughter making contact with her birth mother. She heard a lot of critical, condemning words from them until she went to college; but the tension eased as they thought she was not seeing her mother.

A year later, after graduating from college and taking a job in her hometown, Jennifer picked up the book and read it again. This time she focused on discovering the love language of her parents and mother. She remembered the long embraces her mother would give her every time she arrived and every time she left. She remembered also that often in conversation Christina would reach over and touch her arm. Jennifer had not always felt comfortable with these embraces and touches, but she knew now that physical touch was her birth mom's primary love language.

She concluded that her father's love language was words of affirmation. He had always tried to put a positive spin on things. She never felt as condemned by her dad as by her mother. Even in the worst of times her father would give her affirming words, though often they were negated by his insistence that she not see her mother. Martha's love language was a little more difficult for Jennifer to discover, but she finally concluded it was acts of service.

Speaking Her Family's Love Language

With this information, Jennifer began to respond to the three most significant people in her life by speaking their primary love language every time she encountered them. If she heard that Martha was having guests, she would bake cookies. When she visited she always asked, "What can I do to help you while I'm here?" If her adoptive mother didn't suggest something, she would find something and do it. She began to verbally affirm her father, sometimes in private and sometimes in the presence of her mother. She tried never to leave without having said something positive to him.

When she was with her birth mother, Christina, she entered more fully into the embraces and began taking initiative to put her hand on her mother's back when she passed her on the couch or to kiss her on the cheek after an embrace.

All three of these relationships began to improve. Jennifer began to receive affirming words and found herself feeling genuinely warm toward Martha in spite of those cutting words that had played in her mind for years: "If she loves you so much, why don't you go live with her?" Jennifer realized that because words of affirmation was her love language, Martha's statement had deeply hurt her. That is why she had been unable to erase it from her mind. But now she was hearing affirming words from Martha, and the record of that distant message began to fade. She always knew Martha loved her, and now she was beginning to feel it.

Later Jennifer shared her story at a national singles conference. It was obvious to me that Jennifer's sense of well-being was greatly enhanced by developing a loving relationship with all three parents.

Not everyone has had the kinds of struggles Jennifer encountered with her parents. But many single adults have fractured or broken relationships with their parents. The lack of feeling love from their parents leaves them with an emptiness that cannot be filled by academic or vocational success.

The key takeaway from this chapter is: No matter what has happened between you and your parents, if you will take the initiative to discover their primary love language and begin to speak it, the potential for healing and reconciliation are very real.

On the other hand, you may have a strong, loving relationship with your parents. If so, then discovering their primary love language will simply enhance that relationship.

SIBLINGS: BUILT-IN FRIENDS?

Relationships with siblings are often colored by the events of childhood and adolescence. The nature of the relationship in earlier years influences the relationship as adults. This influence may be positive or negative. If the relationship is positive, then it can only be enhanced by discovering the primary love language of your siblings and speaking that language regularly. If the negative influences of childhood linger into adulthood, then nothing has more potential for healing the hurts of the past than expressing love in the sibling's primary love language.

BRIANNA'S FRECKLES

Brianna was a redheaded, freckle-faced, beautiful single woman who said to me, "When I was growing up, my brother, who is two years older than I, always kidded me about my freckles. He nicknamed me Freckles and introduced me to all his friends by this name. I never liked it, but I didn't make a big deal of it. I would just say, 'My name is Brianna,' and let it go at that. He still introduces me that way even now that we are both grown."

"It's not a big deal, but . . ."
"It's not a big deal, but I don't like it. I wish he would just call me Brianna."

"Have you ever told him?" I asked.

"Not since we were in high school," she said. "I mentioned it a couple of times, but it didn't do any good. Other than that we have a good relationship."

"Do you have any idea what your brother's primary love language is?"

"I think it is quality time," she said. "He's always coming around and wanting to talk with me, especially if he's dating someone new. He wants my advice on what to say. He knows he can always get a glass of tea and sandwich at my place. He'll come by and we'll talk."

"So, do you freely give him your time?" I asked.

"Usually," she said, "though sometimes I have errands to run, and I tell him to make himself at home and I'll be back later. He'll take a nap or watch TV, and we'll pick up our conversation when I get back."

"Do you think your brother genuinely feels loved by you?" I asked.

"I certainly hope so," she said. "Absolutely, if quality time is his love language; I give him a lot of quality time."

"And do you feel loved by your brother?"

"Oh, yes," she said. "My love language is words of affirmation. He's always telling me how smart I am and how much he appreciates my advice."

"Sounds like you have a pretty healthy relationship," I said, "but it would be improved if he would stop calling you Freckles, right?"

She laughed and said, "Yes."

The Big Request

"Then would you be willing to try an experiment with me?" I asked.

"If you think it will help, I'll try anything," she said.

"One night when you are with your brother, tell him that you've been reading a book on communicating love to family members and that you want to ask him a question. The question is this: On a scale of zero to ten, how much do you feel I love you as a sister? If he gives you an eight, nine, or ten, which I am assuming he will, then ask him how much he loves you on a scale of zero to ten. If he gives you a high rating, then tell him you really believe what he says and you sense his love. Therefore, you have one request that would make you feel even more loved.

"Ask him if he would be open to hearing your request. If he says yes (how could he not say yes?), then you simply say, 'I want you to stop introducing me as Freckles. You can call me Freckles if you want to when we are alone, but please don't ever call me Freckles again in public. Just introduce me as your sister, Brianna.'

"He will likely be shocked when you make your request, because he probably has no idea that this still bothers you, but he needs to know. And if he knows, my guess is he'll change, and you will feel even more loved by him."

"Just that straightforward?" she asked. Before I could answer, she said, "That might be hard. I don't want to hurt him, and I don't want him to think I'm silly."

"Is it important to you that he stop introducing you as Freckles?" I asked.

"It really is," she said.

"Then give him a chance. He can't read your mind. It's not silly, and you won't hurt him by asking. You'll be giving him the information he needs to express love to you more effectively."

"I'll try it," she said, and she walked away.

Six months later I got a letter from Brianna. It was a simple letter. At the top was the sketch of a face filled with freckles. Beneath it were these words: "It worked. My brother was very responsive—hasn't introduced me as Freckles in six months. Thanks, Brianna."

Brianna demonstrates a significant principle. If siblings feel loved, they are far more likely to respond to a sincere request. Inasmuch as Brianna was already speaking her brother's primary love language and he already felt loved by her, the simple request was all it took for him to deal with an issue that was important to her, one about which he had not given serious thought in years.

If, on the other hand, her brother had not felt loved by her, she probably would have gotten a different response. When siblings feel unloved, they are likely to take any request as a demand, and their response will be predictably negative. Again, feeling loved makes the difference in the way a person responds to a legitimate request.

BROTHER TO BROTHER

For Steve the road was much more difficult. "My brother and I fought like cats and dogs growing up. I'm one year older than he. I don't know if it was a fight for superiority or something else. We're both grown now, but we still don't have a very close relationship. If I needed help, I wouldn't turn to him."

"Do you want to have a better relationship?" I inquired.

"I do," he said. "We're brothers. Shouldn't brothers at least be cordial to each other? I'm not looking to be 'best buddies' or anything, but I do wish we could be closer.

"Mom and Dad are getting older, and we're going to have to deal with taking care of them a few years down the road. With our relationship like it is, I don't know that we could ever agree on anything. I feel like he still resents me, and I don't know why. I never tried to lord it over him."

I agreed with Steve that it was time for him to make an effort to improve their relationship. I talked with him about the importance of emotional love and that all of us have an emotional love tank: "When the love tank is full and we genuinely feel loved by family members, we tend to have positive, growing relationships. But when the love tank is empty and we do not feel loved by family members, barriers tend to develop between us. We tend to view each other in a negative light and can sometimes even be hostile toward each other."

Moving in the Right Direction

"We're not openly hostile," he said, "but it's definitely not a loving relationship. Tom just got married about two months ago. I don't know if that's going to bring us closer together or not."

"Do you have any idea what your brother's primary love language is?" I asked. Steve had never heard of the love languages and didn't have a clue what I was talking about.

I proceeded to explain the love languages and that each of us has a primary love language that speaks to us more deeply than the other four. I suggested that love is the most powerful way to improve a relationship.

"How would I discover his primary love language?" Steve asked. "I don't see him that much."

I asked Steve several questions about his brother, but his answers shed little light on what his brother's love language might be. So I suggested that, since Tom was recently married, Steve give him and his new wife a copy of *The Five Love Languages*, which focuses on how to keep love alive and thriving in a marriage.

"There are two advantages in doing this," I said. "First, if he and his wife read it, it will enhance their relationship. Secondly, three months after you give them the book, you might ask his wife if she discovered your brother's primary love language." His sister-in-law was probably the best source for discovering Tom's primary love language. Once he got that information from her, he was ready to begin finding ways to speak that love language to Tom. I told him I could almost guarantee that if he started speaking in his brother's primary love language, the relationship between the two of them would begin to change.

Taking the First Step

I didn't see Steve again for about six months. When I saw him next, the first thing he said was, "I discovered my brother's primary language, but I'm having trouble figuring out how to speak it."

"So, what is his love language?" I asked.

"Acts of service. His wife said they both agreed that was his primary love language. But I see Tom so seldom; how can I do acts of service for him?"

"The journey of a thousand miles begins with one step," I said.

"That sounds like philosophy," Steve said.

"It's a good philosophy," I replied. "Would you be willing to try it?"

"Sure, if you will tell me what that one step could be." Steve nodded.

After talking awhile about his brother's lifestyle and interests, we agreed that Steve would offer to keep his brother's dog any weekend that Tom and his new wife wanted to get away. That would definitely be an act of service on Steve's part and something that his brother was likely to appreciate. Even though Steve and his brother had not been close, it would be a logical and helpful offer for his brother and his new sister-in-law. Steve said, "I'll try it," and we parted ways.

About two months passed before I encountered Steve again. This time he said, "I'm scheduled to keep my brother's dog in three weeks!"

"So he accepted your offer?"

"Yeah, he seemed genuinely appreciative that I was willing to do that."

"Good, you're on the road."

"But how many times can I keep the dog," he asked, "and how is that going to improve our relationship?"

The Second Mile: Walking the Dog, Fixing the Deck, Etc.

"Remember, your brother's primary love language is acts of service," I said. "Anytime you do an act of service, it's like pouring love into his love tank. As his love tank begins to fill, he is emotionally drawn to the person who is filling it. So if you keep the dog only once a year, that's like pouring a gallon of love into his love tank. Perhaps he and his wife will take more than one weekend away each year, which may allow for two or three gallons of love."

"But what else can I do?" Steve asked.

"Tell his wife that if your brother needs help on any projects, you would be happy to help him if she would just give you a ring. Then sit back and wait for the phone to ring," I said.

"You make it seem so easy."

"It won't be easy as it seems when you start helping with the projects," I said.

I learned later that within the month Steve was helping his brother replace his deck. Before the year was over, he had mowed his brother's yard twice when he was in the hospital for two weeks, had kept the dog on three weekends, had helped his brother put in a retaining wall for a flower garden, and had dug up some black-eyed Susans from his home garden and transplanted them to his brother's garden.

Steve told me, "I've spent more time with my brother this year than the last fifteen years combined. I feel like we're getting close again. We haven't had any deep conversations about the past. It's just that we both seem more adult, and we're relating to each other as adults."

In it for the Long Haul

"Are you ready for the next level?" I asked.

"Is there another level?" Steve replied.

"Invite him and his wife over for a meal," I said. "You may need your girlfriend's help for that one."

"She's a good cook. We could do that." His eyes lit up like he had just discovered a new toy. "My brother has never been to my place," he said.

"I'll give you another idea," I said. "Does your brother have any interest in sports?"

"He's a NASCAR fan," Steve said, "but he doesn't go very often. He says the tickets are too expensive, so he watches it on television."

"Then buy four tickets and take him to a race," I said.

"Why four?" Steve said.

"Two for your brother and his wife, two for you and your girlfriend," I said.

"His wife would never go to a NASCAR race, and my girlfriend certainly wouldn't."

"Then buy two tickets," I said. "Just you and your brother together for a whole day. Think about it."

"That would definitely be a new level," Steve said.

All these conversations with Steve occurred more than four years ago. He and his brother now have a warm, close, and loving relationship. Steve has a new girlfriend and tells me that he's thinking seriously about marriage. "Be sure you learn to speak her primary love language before you get married," I said.

"I'm already speaking it," he said with a grin.

Steve has demonstrated the power of love to remove barriers and bring family members closer together. Families were designed to be the basic caring unit of society. Learning to speak each other's primary love language in the family turns this design into a reality.

THINGS TO THINK ABOUT

1. List the names of your family members: mother, father, siblings. Using a 0–10 scale (with 0 representing not loved, 5 somewhat loved, and 10 greatly loved), how loved do you feel by each of your family members?

2. Why did you rate each family member as you did? What factors are contributing to the feelings of love?

3. What do you think is each family member's primary love language?

4. How effective do you think you have been in speaking their primary love languages? Answer the question by listing each family member's name and writing a number from the 0–10 scale (0 meaning you don't know it, 5 expressing it occasionally, and 10 consistently speaking the language).

5. Use the chart on the next page to map out a strategy for expressing love to your family members more effectively in the weeks ahead.

HOW TO SAY "I LOVE YOU" TO MY FAMILY

List below each member of your family and his or her love language. Then write a few ways to show love for each of them. Reflect on the suggestions in this chapter for ideas.

Name: _____ *Love Language*: _____
My love response:_____
_____
_____
_____

Name: _____ *Love Language*: _____
My love response:_____
_____
_____
_____

Name: _____ *Love Language*: _____
My love response:_____
_____
_____
_____

Name: _____ *Love Language*: _____
My love response:_____
_____
_____
_____

10

dating relationships—part 1:

LOVE LANGUAGES AND
YOUR SPECIAL SOMEONE

I HAVE MET MANY SINGLES who have given up on dating. They find it to be a road strewn with heartache, physical frustration, misunderstanding, and untold anxiety, all of which add up to a "why bother?" attitude. Yet, for others, the very idea of not dating sounds unnatural. What are the factors that must be considered here?

First, let me remind you that dating is not a universal practice. In many cultures, literate and illiterate alike, the very idea of a guy and a girl arranging a series of times to get together, for whatever purpose, would be considered taboo. These cultures have a long history of many stable marriages. Therefore, dating is not the necessary part of the marriage process that we generally assume it to be.

However, having said that, we must be realistic and admit that dating is a very integral part of Western culture. In fact, some have referred to dating as "America's Favorite Tribal Custom." The pitfalls in the system do not mean that the process itself is necessarily evil. On the contrary, it may be one of the most healthy and beneficial social systems in our entire society.

WHAT'S THE POINT?

The reason many singles have failed in the dating game is that they have never clearly understood their objectives. If you ask a group of singles, "Why are you dating?" the answers would range all the way from "to have a good time" to "to find a mate." In some general sense we know that the end of all of this may lead us to marriage, but we are not clear as to other specific objectives. Let me list a few and suggest that you add to the list as you give thought to your own personal objectives.

1. Develop Wholesome Interactions with the Opposite Sex

One of the purposes of dating is to get to know members of the opposite sex and to learn to relate to them as individual people. Half of the world is made up of the opposite sex. If I fail to learn the art of building wholesome relationships with "the other half," I have immediately and considerably limited my horizons. God made us male and female, and it is His desire that we relate to each other as fellow creatures who share His image. Our differences are numerous, but our basic needs are the same. If we are to serve people, which is life's highest calling, then we must know them—male and female. Relationships cannot be built without some kind of social interaction. In Western culture, dating provides the setting for such interaction.

One of our chief stumbling blocks to healthy dating relationships is that we have been trained to view each other as sex objects. Over fifty years ago psychologist Erich Fromm wrote, "What most people in our culture mean by being lovable is essentially a mixture between being popular and having sex appeal."[1] With a proliferation of digital cable, On-Demand movies, and the Internet as a lifestyle, this perception of others as sex objects has become deeply ingrained in our thinking.

For some single women their unspoken (or maybe even spoken) lifestyle objective is to "turn the heads" of the men they encounter. And many men are happy to turn their heads. Many also proceed further and give their attention to the wide array of pornographic materials that are now readily available anywhere there is an Internet connection. These individuals often find themselves addicted to this impersonal, disconnected perception of members of the opposite sex. When this becomes a fixed perception, then one ceases in the truest sense to be human. He or she becomes like an animal playing with his toys or allowing one's self to be a toy with which another animal plays.

2. Learn about the Person, Personality, and Philosophy

Dating provides an opportunity to break down the perceptions of each other that the world has built up, and to learn to see others as persons rather than objects. It is in dating that we can learn names, personalities, and philosophies. These are the qualities of personhood. The name identifies us as a unique person. The personality reveals the nature of our uniqueness. And the philosophy reveals the values by which we live our lives. All of these are discovered, not as we stand back and view each other as objects, but as we come close and begin to interact more personally with each other.

It is in dating that we discover every woman has a mother and a father, and so does every man. Known or unknown, living or dead, our parents have influenced us and thus profoundly affected who we are. We are all connected with our past. In the dating relationship we have the potential for excavating these roots. Every person has a personal history that has also greatly influenced him or her. In the context of dating, these histories are shared.

Our society increasingly pushes us to live in cocoons of cubicles, attached garages, iPod headphones, and lonely (non-carpool lane) com-

THE FIVE LOVE LANGUAGES — SINGLES EDITION

mutes. This isolation has brought us to growing levels of loneliness, emptiness, and sometimes desperation. However, this isolation need not be a permanent prison. Dating is an acceptable way of breaking out of isolation and connecting with others.

Abby, a very reserved, almost shy single, did not date in high school and only dated twice in college. However, upon graduation and landing her first job, she began to attend a singles group in a local church. She took the opportunity to go out for dessert with a smaller group and in this context met Brent. They had been dating for three months when Abby said to me, "I don't know why I waited so long to start dating. It feels so good to be getting to know someone else and letting him know me." Abby has taken a giant step in getting to know someone as a person.

3. See Our Own Strengths and Weaknesses

A third purpose of dating is to aid in the development of one's own personality. All of us are in process. Someone once suggested to me that we ought to wear signs around our necks reading: "Under Construction."

As we relate to others in the dating context, we begin to exhibit various personality traits. This provokes healthy self-analysis and brings greater self-understanding. We recognize that some traits are more desirable than others. We come to see our own strengths and weaknesses. The acknowledgement of a weakness is the first step toward growth.

All of us have strengths and weaknesses in our personalities. No one is perfect. Maturity is not flawlessness. However, we are never to be satisfied with our present status of development. If we are overly withdrawn we cannot minister freely to others. If, on the other hand, we are overly talkative we may overwhelm those we would like to help. Relating to someone in a dating relationship has a way of letting us see ourselves and cooperate in God's plan of growth for our lives.

A number of years ago a very talkative young man said to me, "I never realized how obnoxious I was until I dated Sally. She talks all the time, and it drives me up the wall." The light had dawned; his eyes were opened. In Sally he saw his own weakness and was mature enough to take steps toward growth.

For him this meant curbing his speech and developing his listening skills. His was a prescription written in the first century by one of the apostles in the early Christian church: "My dear brothers, take note of this: Everyone should be quick to listen, slow to speak and slow to become angry."[2] What we dislike in others is often a weakness in our own lives. Dating can help us see ourselves realistically.

Changing personality weaknesses is not always easy. Abby, whom we met earlier, realized that her shyness was detrimental in building relationships with others. Upon graduation from college, she decided to get personal counseling. It was here that she gained the insight and encouragement to take steps in the right direction. The first of those was to attend a singles group at a local church. The second was to push herself to go out with a smaller group for dessert. What was more difficult for Abby was learning how to share her ideas in that small group, to talk about herself, and to let people know about her college experience and her present vocation.

It took about six months for her to develop the courage to ask Brent over for dinner, which was the first step in developing their relationship.

Once they started dating, Abby sensed that Brent was someone she could trust. With encouragement from her counselor, she began to share with Brent the details of her history. His interest in listening encouraged her to proceed. In the early stages, her counselor encouraged her to write down the things that she would tell Brent that night and the questions she would ask him about his life. By writing it down beforehand, Abby

THE FIVE LOVE LANGUAGES — SINGLES EDITION

had the courage to follow through. Change takes effort, but it is effort well invested.

4. Practice Serving Others

A fourth purpose of dating is that it provides an opportunity to serve others. History is replete with examples of men and women who discovered that humanity's greatest contribution is in giving to others. Who does not know of Mother Teresa? Her name is synonymous with service. In Africa there was Albert Schweitzer, and in India, Mohandas Gandhi. Most people who have studied the life of Jesus of Nazareth agree that His life can be summarized by His simple act of washing the feet of His disciples. He Himself said, "[I] did not come to be served, but to serve, and to give [My] life as a ransom for many."[3] He instructed His followers, "Whoever wants to become great among you must be your servant."[4] True greatness is expressed in serving.

I do not mean to convey the idea that dating should be done in a spirit of martyrdom — "Poor ol' me. I have to do this service as my duty," or "If I serve this guy, maybe he will like me." Ministry (serving) is different from martyrdom. Ministry is something we do for others, whereas martyrdom is something others bring upon us.

Dating is always a two-way street. Certainly we receive something from the relationship, but we are also to be contributing to the life of the person we are dating. Immeasurable good could be accomplished if we could see service as one of the purposes of dating. Many a reserved fellow could be "drawn out" by the wise questions of a dating partner. Many a hothead could be calmed by the truth spoken in love.

Taking ministry seriously may change your attitude towards dating. You have been trained to "put your best foot forward" so that the other person will be impressed by you. Consequently, you may have been reluctant to speak to your partner's weaknesses, fearing he or she would walk away from you. Genuine service demands that we speak the truth in love. We do not serve each other by avoiding one another's weaknesses.

Fortunately, not all of our service involves pointing out the weaknesses of our dating partners. Often we help them simply by listening as they share their struggles. Empathetic listening is an awesome medication for the hurting heart. Jim was dating Tricia when her father died of a heart attack. They had only been dating a few weeks, but Jim sensed that she wanted him to be with her. So he sat with the family for the memorial service and accompanied Tricia to the burial. The next few weeks he often asked her questions about her father and let her talk freely of her memories.

In doing this, Jim was helping Tricia work through the grief that so deeply pained her. Had they not been dating, he would not have had this opportunity to serve, which was extremely helpful for Tricia.

5. Discover the Person We Will Marry

Another obvious purpose of dating is to help us discover the kind of person we will marry. As noted earlier, in some cultures marriages are arranged. Contracts are drawn up between respective families. The choice is made on the basis of social, financial, or religious considerations. The couple is supposed to develop love once they are married. In Western culture the process is left to the individuals involved. Frankly, I prefer this process. Dating is designed to help us gain a realistic idea of the kind of person we need as a marriage partner.

Dating people with differing personalities gives us criteria for making wise judgments. Someone who has limited dating experience may, after marriage, be plagued with thoughts like: "What are other women/ men like?" or "Would I have had a better marriage with another type of mate?" These questions may come to all couples, especially when there is trouble in the marriage. But the individual who looks back on a well-rounded social life before marriage is better equipped to answer these questions. He is not as likely to build a dream world, because experience has taught him that all of us are imperfect.

What could be more difficult than finding someone with whom we can live in harmony and fulfillment for the next fifty years? The variables are great. The old idea is that opposites attract. There is truth to that, but opposites may also repel. That is why couples can be so attracted before marriage and so disillusioned afterwards. The reality is the more similar we are, the fewer conflicts we will have. Similarity is especially important when it comes to the bigger issues of life: values, spirituality, morals, whether or not to have children, how many children to have, and vocational goals. Dating provides the context for exploring answers to these questions and determining our suitability for marriage.

WHAT ABOUT THE LOVE LANGUAGES?

Probably you've noticed that up until now we haven't discussed love as an element in the dating process. The reason for that should be obvious. Genuine love interfaces with all the ideas we have discussed about dating. An attitude of love should motivate you to want to relate to others as persons rather than objects, to develop your own personality so you can reach your potential for good in the world, and to serve your dating partner and seek to encourage that person to reach his/her potential. In seeking a mate, love is the foundational motivation, which doesn't just lead to a wedding, but to a successful marriage.

If this is true, then learning to express love in a language your dating partner will understand becomes critical. When the dating partner feels loved, he or she is much more likely to be open to an authentic relationship. Your dating relationships will be enhanced if you learn to speak the primary love language of the person you are dating.

BEYOND THE TINGLES: SHELLEY AND NEIL

Shelley and Neil met each other near the end of their freshman year in college and had been dating for about two and a half years. They were both seniors and were contemplating graduate school. They were also talking seriously about their relationship.

"I feel like we are losing something," Neil told me. "Our relationship has always been good, but it's like the excitement is gone. At one time we had talked about getting married after graduation, but now we're not sure. If you've got time, we'd like to sit down and talk with you about it."

Two weeks later Shelley and Neil came to my office. After spending an hour listening to their story, it seemed like they were a couple who had the foundation for a lasting relationship. But to check out my own perceptions I suggested that they take a personality inventory. Such inventories involve answering a series of questions in private. The inventories are then scored and a counselor interprets the results. Neil and Shelley agreed, and when their profile came back it indicated that they were highly compatible in all the basic areas required for a stable marriage.

With this information in hand, I explained to them what I thought had happened in their relationship. I reviewed the nature of the "in love" experience: how it begins with the "tingles" and develops into an emotional obsession where the person is viewed through rose-colored glasses and appears to be perfect. I reminded them that this is one of the highest emotional experiences ever between two people. I also reminded them that it is temporary—gone within two years. When we come off this emotional obsession, we begin to view each other in more realistic terms. We see their weaknesses as well as their strengths. We realize they are not perfect. This is when the couple begins to feel like love is slipping away from them.

Now they must be much more intentional in their behavior. The "in love" stage of marriage requires little effort. In fact, "falling in love" was not a conscious choice. Whatever we do in the "in love" state requires little discipline or conscious effort on our part. The long phone calls we make to each other, the money we spend traveling to see each other, the gifts we give, and the ridiculous work projects we do are nothing to us. As the instinctual nature of a bird dictates the building of a nest, so the instinctual nature of the "in love" experience pushes us along in our euphoria. But when the euphoria has run its course, we must take responsibility for our behavior. Love, at this point, becomes a choice.

This is where knowledge of the five love languages becomes exceedingly important. If we understand the five fundamental languages of love, and understand that each of us speaks a different one, then we can become intentional in expressing love to our dating partner. When we do this, they continue to feel our love even though the euphoria and distorted thinking of the "in love" stage has vanished.

I also shared with Shelley and Neil that this is the stage in a relationship where we can more easily take an honest look at the important factors in our relationship: values, morals, spirituality, vocational goals, and marriage. I reminded them that both my perception of their relationship and the results shown on the personality inventory indicated they had strong similarities in all the basic areas required for a solid marital relationship.

"Obviously, it's not my call as to whether you continue your relationship," I said. "That is something only the two of you can decide, but I do think you have the foundation for a lifelong relationship. If you can discover and speak each other's primary love language, you will rediscover the spark in your relationship." I could tell they were up for the challenge.

Three months later they stopped by my office, not for counseling, but to share with me that they were now engaged and planning to be married after graduation. "The love languages worked for us," Neil said. "The spark is back, and we know we want to get married."

Shelley added, "We shared your love language book with my parents, and we've seen the spark return to their marriage. Thanks so much for taking time with us."

"Send me an invitation to the wedding," I said. "If I'm free, I'll come."

TO MARRY OR NOT TO MARRY?

The experience of "falling in love" is not a foundation for a happy marriage. It is highly possible to be "in love" with someone you should not marry. In fact, you will probably feel the "tingles" for almost everyone you date. It is the "tingles" that motivate us to want to spend time with the other person. As you date, sometimes the "tingles" dissipate quickly, and the relationship never gets off the ground. On the other hand, the "tingles" may develop into the emotional obsession I am calling the experience of "falling in love." None of this requires much effort or thought. All you did was show up, and the emotions took over. However, a marital relationship designed to last a lifetime requires more than these euphoric, obsessive feelings.

A Time to Talk About the Real Stuff

We must not allow the euphoria to blind us from seeing the glaring differences between us on the fundamental issues. That is why I have emphasized such things as values, morals, spirituality, social interests, vocational visions, and the desire or lack of desire to have children. Dating provides the context for serious discussion about these issues if we are not blinded by the exhilaration of it all. If we are too far apart on these fundamental issues, we should be wise enough to express appreciation for the contribution made to the other's life and then go our separate ways. To marry in the height of the "in love" euphoria and ignore these more fundamental issues is to set one's self up for a painful and difficult marriage.

Lindsey was wise enough to see this. She and her fiancé, Marcus, were assigned the responsibility during a conference of taking me to dinner one evening. In the course of our conversation she shared with me how helpful *The Five Love Languages* had been to her. "I had been dating another guy for about a year before I met Marcus," she said. "I really felt loved. I guess maybe I was 'in love' with him. But when Marcus came along there was something different about him. It wasn't so much the emotions. I admired who he was. I admired his character and the way he invested his life working with troubled kids at the local boys' club.

"After we started dating it bothered me that I didn't have the same emotional feelings for him that I had for my former boyfriend. He was much more the kind of person I wanted to marry, but I couldn't figure why I was still having such strong feelings for the other guy. Then one day I was reading your book on love languages. My mother had loaned me her copy. It was written for married couples, but it made sense to me.

"When I finished reading, it dawned on me that my love language was physical touch, and the reason I still had feelings for my former boyfriend was that he was a toucher. He would put his arm around me at movies. He would hold hands every time we got out of the car to go somewhere. He would hug me and kiss me every time we parted, whereas Marcus was not a toucher. At least at that stage in our relationship he was not touching me very much.

"I guess he didn't want the physical part of our relationship to become the main thing, so he was holding back. And I was not feeling emotionally close to him. When we talked about it and Marcus explained why he was not being more physically responsive, I appreciated his efforts to hold back on physical touching until we got to know each other better.

"Of course, now he's touching me," she said, laughing. "My love tank is running over."

"I always wanted to touch her," Marcus said. "In the past I had relationships where physical touch was about all we had in common. I didn't want that to be true in this relationship. I wanted to get to know her as a person and make sure that we had real interest in each other."

A Commitment to Core Beliefs

"I really appreciate that about him," Lindsey said. "The more I got to know him, the more I knew he was the kind of person I wanted to marry. When the touches finally came, I knew that he was the one I wanted to hug and kiss me for the rest of my life. That's why I said yes when he asked me to marry him."

Good marriages are built on a combination of emotional love and a common commitment to a core of beliefs about what is most important and what we wish to do with our lives. Speaking each other's primary love language creates the emotional climate where these beliefs can be fleshed out in daily life.

THINGS TO THINK ABOUT

As you reflect upon your present and past dating relationships, answer the following questions:

1. To what degree did I view him/her as a person rather than an object?

2. How well did I discover his/her personality, history, values, morals, and spiritual beliefs?

3. What discoveries did I make about myself in this dating relationship?

4. What positive changes did I make?

5. In what ways did I help my dating partner?

6. How well did I do in empathetic listening and in confronting weaknesses?

7. Why did I decide to marry or not marry this person?

8. If we had known each other's primary love language, what difference might this have made in our relationship?

11

dating relationships—part 2:

SHOULD LOVE
LEAD TO MARRIAGE?

I WAS SITTING at my desk one Saturday morning, sorting papers, when I got a call from Mark. We've known each other for over thirty years. I participated in the weddings of his children. I presided over the funeral of his wife five years earlier. I had walked with Mark through the pain of grief, but I could tell by the tone of his voice that something was different. It didn't take long to figure out what was going on. After asking the usual "Let's catch up" questions, he said, "I'm calling to let you know that I'm getting married."

"Married?" I exclaimed. "When?"

"On Christmas Day," he replied. "All the kids and grandkids will be here, so we decided that would be a good time for the wedding."

"Well, congratulations!" I said. "I'm happy for you."

"I would like for you to be a part of the ceremony," he said. "We're going to get married at her church, and her pastor will be leading things. But we both want you to be involved as well."

"I'd be honored," I said.

Mark and I finished our conversation, and then I walked upstairs to give my wife the good news. "I'm surprised he's waited this long," she said matter-of-factly. We both knew Mark had been dating Sylvia for about three years. Her husband passed away two months before Mark's wife did. She had strong Christian commitments and was quite active in community life. Sylvia and Mark had a lot in common.

Both Karolyn and I felt good about their relationship. Because of their age and past experience, neither Mark nor Sylvia felt the need for premarital counseling. They were fairly happy in their first marriages and assumed they would be happily married again.

Two years later, Mark called again. His tone was much more somber: "I think we need help," he said. "We've got some pretty severe disagreements, and we just can't get on the same page. Maybe I made a mistake in getting married again. It seems that neither one of us is very happy."

Over the next three months, I met regularly with Mark and Sylvia. We worked our way through a number of conflicts regarding children, furniture, money, retirement, vehicles, and church. However, at the root of all their unresolved conflicts was an empty love tank. Neither of them felt loved by the other. They had dated for three years, so the in-love obsession had run its course before they got married. But because they had so much in common and enjoyed being with each other, they didn't see that as a problem. They knew from past experience that the in-love obsession was temporary. However, two years after the wedding, their differences (which seldom surfaced before marriage) became divisive. And the lack of emotional love created a climate of tension. They did not yell and scream at each other; they were much too mature for that, but both admitted that they were living with a high level of emotional frustration.

A HARDWORKING MAN WHO DIDN'T "GET IT"

Sylvia's primary love language was quality time. Before marriage, Mark spoke her love language fluently. On their dates, he gave her his undivided attention. She felt genuinely loved by him even after the in-love obsession faded. However, after the wedding, she discovered that living with Mark was far different from dating Mark. He was a super-active person, and there were always "things to be done." There were lawns to be mowed, shrubbery to be trimmed, leaves to be blown, cars to be washed, walls to be painted, carpet to be replaced. There was always a project.

"He is a hardworking man," said Sylvia. "The problem is that he never has any time for me. It's not that I don't appreciate what he does. I do, but what good is it if we don't have time for each other?"

On the other hand, Mark really didn't get it. "I don't understand her," he said. "Most women would be glad to have a husband like me. How can she say I don't love her?"

Instead of answering Mark's question prematurely, I turned the conversation by asking, "On a scale of zero to ten, how much love do you feel coming from Sylvia?"

He was silent for a moment and then said, "About zero right now. All she ever does is criticize me. I never thought it would come to this. Before we got married, she was always so positive. When I painted the living room at her house and replaced the windows in her bedroom, she couldn't say enough about how great I was. Now I do the same thing in our house and it doesn't count for anything."

Mark's primary love language was words of affirmation.

Instead of explaining, I gave them a copy of *The Five Love Languages* and said, "The answer to your marriage is in this book. I want you to read it carefully, and two weeks from today I want you to tell me why neither of you feel loved." I don't think either of them was very impressed with my approach, but they both agreed to read the book.

Two weeks later the atmosphere was very different. They walked into my office smiling. "Now we know why you wanted us to read this book before we got married," Sylvia said. "I wish we had listened to you."

I resisted the urge to say, "I wish you had also." Instead, I said, "You can't relive the past two years, but you can make the future very different."

FILLING SYLVIA'S LOVE TANK

"So, what is Sylvia's love language?" I asked Mark.

"Quality time, without a doubt," he said. "For two years, I've been doing projects when she needed me to sit on the couch and talk with her, take drives in the country, and walk around the neighborhood after dinner. I was always too busy for those things. Now I realize that I was wrong. Because I didn't speak her love language, she did the only thing she knew to do — she grumbled."

"And what is your love language?" I asked.

"My primary love language is words of affirmation, which is why her complaining hurt me so deeply. It was like a knife to my heart."

"I realize now what I did," Sylvia said. "My love tank was so empty. I didn't even know I had a love tank, so I certainly didn't realize that it was empty. I did what was natural for me; I tried to express my need. I see now that it came across as condemning him. Instead of affirming him for all the good things he was doing, I criticized him because he was not meeting my deeper needs. We both apologized to each other, and we know the future is going to be different," she said.

"I promised her we will have a date night every week," Mark said. "And we will take a walk after dinner at least one night a week, maybe two. And every three months, we're going to take a weekend trip together."

"It's like we are starting our marriage over again," Sylvia said, "only this time, we know how to love each other. Mark is one of the hardest-working men I've ever known. And from now on, I'm going to make sure he knows I appreciate that about him."

It's been over a decade now since that conversation with Mark and Sylvia. Sylvia recently said to me, "I can't thank you enough for the time you spent with us. It literally saved our marriage," and Mark told me, "I want you to know that I could not be happier."

In the midst of crisis Mark and Sylvia discovered something that could have been figured out while they were dating. Unfortunately they did what thousands of people do—assume that the love relationship will continue after marriage without much (or any) effort. Before marriage they were speaking each other's love language but were not conscious of what they were doing. The dating context made it easy for Mark to give Sylvia quality time. She was the focus of his attention while they were together. Because she felt loved, it was easy for her to give him affirming words.

If romantic love leads to marriage, be sure you continue to speak your partner's love language. Remember, this takes real work—but it's worth the effort. The marriage context is very different from the dating context. In the normalcy of married life, Mark busied himself with things he thought would be important to her, missing the most important thing— quality time. When Sylvia ceased to give him affirming words, his love tank drained quickly. Without emotional love, their differences became battlefields, and both of them questioned the wisdom of their marriage. And without an understanding of the nature of love, their marriage would undoubtedly have ended in divorce.

WHY MARRY?

What Most of Us Seek

Well, if it's so hard and the odds aren't so good, this question might come up: why bother? With so many marriages ending in divorce, why take the risk? The simple answer is that we all desire to love and be loved uniquely, and that leads most of us into a covenant marriage relationship. Despite the rise in divorce, cohabitation, and unwed parenthood, marriage remains an aspiration of the vast majority of men and women. A recent survey found that 93 percent of Americans "rate 'having a happy marriage' as either one of the most important, or very important objectives."[1]

With this desire, however, there are realistic fears. One research project that explored the attitude of today's college students concluded, "They are desperate to have only one marriage, and they want it to be happy. They don't know whether this is possible anymore."[2]

If college students — and other single adults — can understand the nature of love and how to express it effectively, they can have the "happy marriages" they desire. And so, my plea to every single who reads this book is to: (1) apply these principles in every dating relationship, (2) accept the thrill of the in-love obsession for what it is — exciting but temporary, and (3) commit yourself to purposeful love expressed in the other person's primary love language.

When those in dating relationships do these things, they can then assess the other aspects of life that will help them make a wise decision about marriage.

Seven Common Purposes

Before we explore those "other aspects," perhaps we ought to pause long enough to ask: "What is the purpose of marriage?" If you ask a dozen friends that question, you may receive a dozen answers. Here are some of the answers I received from the many single adults I have interacted with over the years:

1. Companionship
2. Sex
3. Love
4. To provide a home for children
5. Social acceptance
6. Economic advantage
7. Security

But can't these objectives be accomplished outside of marriage? Yes. Although abundant research has indicated that married people are happier, healthier, and better off financially.[3] Still, the purpose of marriage runs deeper than any of these seven goals.

A Deeper Purpose

In the ancient biblical account of Creation, God says of Adam, "It is not good for the man to be alone." God's answer to man's need was "I will make a helper suitable for him."[4] The Hebrew word for suitable literally means "face-to-face." The picture is that God created one with whom man could have a face-to-face relationship. It speaks of that kind of in-depth, personal relationship whereby the two are united in an unbreakable union that satisfies the deepest longings of the human heart.

Marriage is God's answer for humanity's deepest need—union of life with another. Indeed, that same ancient account of creation says of Adam and Eve, "They will become one flesh."[5]

Man's psychological history is replete with his desire for connection. I believe that marriage is designed to be the most intimate of all human relationships. The husband and wife are going to share life intellectually, emotionally, socially, physically, and spiritually, and they are going to share life to such a degree that they become "one flesh." This does not mean that married couples lose their individuality, but it does mean that they have a deep sense of unity.

This kind of union does not come without a deep and enduring commitment. Marriage is not a contract to make sexual relationships legal. It is not merely a social institution to provide for the care of children. It is not merely a psychological clinic where we gain the emotional support we need. It is not a means of gaining social status or economic security. The ultimate purpose of marriage is not even achieved when it is the vehicle for love and companionship, as valuable as these are.

The supreme purpose of marriage is the union of a man and woman at the deepest possible level and in all areas of life, which in turn brings the greatest possible sense of fulfillment to the couple and best serves the purposes of God for their lives.

THE NATURE OF MARITAL UNITY

If the goal of marriage is the deep union of two individuals in every area of life, then what implications does this goal have for an individual who is contemplating marriage? The act of getting married does not just give a couple this kind of unity. There is a difference between "being united" and "unity."

If our goal is oneness, then the key question before marriage ought to be "What reasons do we have for believing that we can become one?" As we examine the intellectual, social, emotional, spiritual, and physical areas of life, what do we find? Do we hold enough in common in these areas to provide a foundation for unity? No house should be built without a suitable foundation. Likewise, no marriage should be initiated until the couple has explored their foundation.

What does this mean in a practical sense? It means that couples thinking of marriage ought to spend time discussing each basic area of life in order to determine who they are. I have encountered quite a few married couples who have very little understanding of each other's intellectual interests. Many marry with only a superficial understanding of each other's personality or emotional makeup. Others marry thinking that religious and moral values are unimportant, and therefore give them little consideration. If you want an intimate marriage, doesn't it make sense to build a strong foundation? The remaining pages of this chapter are for singles in dating relationships who want to evaluate the foundations of their relationships (while trying to speak their partner's love language) as they consider marriage.

Intellectual Unity

To properly explore the foundation of intellectual unity, you need to get very practical. Try this: Set aside specific dating time to discuss with each other the kinds of books you read. This reveals something of your intellectual interest. If one of you doesn't really read books, this also is revealing. Do you read the newspaper regularly? What magazines do you read? What kind of TV shows do you enjoy most? Which Web sites do you frequent? The answer to all these questions will indicate something of your intellectual interests.

Grades in school and the amount of education each of you has should also be considered. This does not mean that you must have the same areas of intellectual interests, but you ought to be able to communicate with each other on the same intellectual plane. Many couples awaken a short time after they get married to discover that this area of life was off-limits because of an inability to understand each other. They never really even considered it before marriage.

I'm not talking about perfection here, but I am talking about building foundations. Do you hold enough in common intellectually to have a basis for growth? This may be best answered by attempting some growth exercises. Agree to read the same book and spend some quality time discussing its concepts. Once a week read the headline article at your news website of choice and discuss its merits and implications. This will reveal a great deal regarding your present status and potential for future growth in intellectual intimacy.

Social Unity

We are all social creatures, but our social interests will often differ greatly. You owe it to yourself and each other to explore the foundation. Is he a sports fan? How many hours each week does he spend watching ESPN? (Do you think this is going to change after marriage?) What are your musical interests? What about opera ... ballet ... gospel songs? (Did you cringe reading any of those? What about your significant other?) I remember the young wife who said, "He wants to have that dumb country-and-western music on all the time, and I can't stand it!" It never seemed important before marriage. I wonder why? Could it have been the "in love" obsession?

What kinds of recreational activities do you enjoy? Have you ever heard of "golf widows"? Do you enjoy parties, and if so, what kind of parties? These are questions that you can't afford not to answer.

"Do we have to have the same social interests?" you ask. No, but you must have a foundation for unity. Do you hold enough in common that you can begin to grow together? Such social growth ought to begin before marriage. If it doesn't, it's not likely to begin afterward. Stretch yourself. Go to things you haven't learned to enjoy before. See if you can learn to enjoy some of the same things. If you find that you are marching in two different directions socially, remember that the goal of marriage is unity. Ask yourself, *If he never changes his present social interest, will I be happy to live with him the rest of my life?*

What about your personality? Could you write a descriptive paragraph about the kind of person you are? Then why not do it? And have your prospective mate do the same. Share these with each other and discuss your self-concept as compared with how you appear to others.

Do you understand each other well enough to believe that you can work as a team? Sure, your personality can complement his, but does he want to be complemented?

What clashes have you had in your dating relationship? What do you see as potential problem areas when you think of living life together? Discuss these openly. Can you make progress in overcoming these difficulties before marriage? If it is an unresolved problem before marriage, it will be magnified after marriage.

This does not mean that your personalities should be identical—that could make for a pretty boring marriage. There should, however, be a basic understanding of each other's personality and some idea of how you will relate to each other. Personality clashes will not be resolved by merely getting married.

Emotional Unity

Because of the euphoria of the "in love" experience, many couples feel like they have genuine emotional intimacy. As one person said to me, "This is the strongest part of our relationship. We really connect emotionally." However, when the euphoria subsides, some couples discover that the foundation for emotional intimacy is extremely weak. They experience feelings of estrangement and distance. "I don't know how I could have felt so close to him six months ago when today I feel like I don't even know him," one recent bride confided.

What is emotional intimacy? It is that deep sense of being connected to one another. It is feeling *loved, respected*, and *appreciated*, while at the same time seeking to reciprocate.

To feel loved is to have the sense that the other person genuinely cares about your well-being. Respect has to do with feeling that your potential spouse has positive regard for your personhood, intellect, abilities, and personality. Appreciation is the inner sense that your partner values your contribution to the relationship. Let's explore these three ingredients to emotional unity.

Evidence of genuine love includes speaking each other's primary love language consistently. After you have discussed the concepts in this book and discovered each other's love language, ask yourself: How fluently do you speak it? How much are you—and your partner—trying to speak each other's love languages?

Respect begins with this attitude: "I acknowledge that you are a creature of extreme worth. God has endowed you with certain abilities and emotions. Therefore I respect you as a person. I will not desecrate your worth by making critical remarks about your intellect, your judgment, or your logic. I will seek to understand you and grant you the freedom to think differently from the way I think and to experience emotions that I may not experience." Respect means that you give the other person the freedom to be an individual. You must also ask this question: Does the person you are considering as a spouse respect you? You can tell by the way they treat your ideas, emotions, and dreams.

The third element of emotional unity is the sense of being appreciated. When we express appreciation, it means that we recognize the value of the other person's contribution to our relationship. Each of us expends our energy and abilities in ways that benefit our relationship. To sense that our potential mate recognizes our efforts and appreciates them builds emotional intimacy between the two of us.

This appreciation can look like complimenting each other. She might say, "Thanks for calling me when you realized you were going to be late. It means a lot to me that you were thinking about me." Or, "Thanks for inviting me over for a meal. I know how much time and energy it takes to prepare a meal like this. I want you to know that I really appreciate your hard work, and the meal was delicious." Such statements communicate appreciation. If, on the other hand, your thoughtful acts go unnoticed, you may begin to feel unappreciated, and emotional distance develops between the two of you.

Appreciation may also focus on abilities: "I love to hear you sing. You are so talented." Or personality: "I am so grateful for your positive spirit about things. I know you were disappointed last night when I had to cancel our date, but it made me feel so much better when you told me you understood." Appreciation requires concentration. First of all, I must be observant of the other person's actions, words, attitudes, and personality. Then, I must take initiative to express my gratitude.

If there is genuine love, respect, and appreciation, then you will experience emotional unity. Discuss these three ingredients before marriage. Share with each other what makes you feel loved, respected, and appreciated.[6] The degree to which you develop emotional unity before marriage will set the pace for your intimacy after marriage.

Spiritual Unity

Spiritual foundations are often the least excavated, even by couples who attend church regularly. Many married couples find that their greatest disappointment in marriage is that there is so little unity in this area.

"We never pray together," said one wife. "Church is like something we do individually. Even though we sit together, we never discuss what we experience," said another. Instead of unity, there is growing isolation, the exact opposite of what we desired in marriage.

Too many premarital discussions on religion deal only with church attendance and other external matters. They fail to grapple with the most basic and important issues: "Is your fiancé a Christian?" I often ask. The normal reply is "Oh, yes, he's a member at St. Mark's."

I am not talking about church membership, charitable giving, or family tradition. I am talking about the spiritual foundation for marriage. Do you each agree that there is an infinite, personal God? Do you know this God? These questions get to the heart of the matter.

It is not enough to be associated with similar religious organizations. It is a matter of personal beliefs. For example, if the man has a deep commitment to Jesus Christ as Lord and senses God's direction into missions work, but the woman has visions of summer cottages, BMWs, and full-time cleaning help, do they have an adequate foundation for marriage?

Here are legitimate questions to consider: Do your hearts beat together spiritually? Are you encouraging each other in spiritual growth, or is one gently but consistently pulling in the opposite direction? Spiritual foundations are important. In fact, they are the most important because they influence all other areas of life and unity.

Physical Unity

If you are physically attracted to each other, you probably have the foundation for physical unity. But there is an interesting fact about sexual unity: it can't be separated from emotional, spiritual, and social unity. In fact, the problems that develop in the sexual aspect of marriage almost always have their root in one of these other areas. Physical incompatibility is almost nonexistent. The problem lies in other areas—it just makes itself known in the sexual area.

There are a few things that ought to be done in order to determine the nature of the foundation in this area of life. If you are headed toward marriage, a thorough physical examination for both partners is essential. With nineteen million new cases of sexually transmitted diseases each year[7]—almost half among those ages fifteen to twenty-four—entering marriage without a physical examination is like playing Russian roulette. Then you have to realistically face the implications of such a disease. For some sexually transmitted diseases there are no cures, only medications to help manage the symptoms. Are you willing to live with this reality in a marriage partner?

The 1960s sexual revolution ushered in a great divide between the exercise of sexuality and the institution of marriage. The "liberating" message was that the two no longer needed each other. The sexual revolution was supposed to set sex and its participants free. It's been nearly half a century and, as one college student concluded, "The sexual revolution is over, and everyone lost."[8] Reformers proposed that the sexual revolution would relieve the repression of the previous era. Instead, the revolution created its own kind of slavery.

As a consequence of this glamorized lifestyle, a fulfilling sex life is more elusive to the present generation than ever. The research indicates: "monogamous individuals committed to one lifetime partner are the most physically and emotionally satisfied people sexually."[9]

I believe that most people who engage in sexual relationships outside of marriage do so out of a sincere desire to find intimacy. Unfortunately, sexual intercourse does not create intimacy. Sex outside of marriage often sidetracks the process of building intimacy and becomes itself a source of great pain physically and emotionally. I recognize that many single adults who read this book have experienced that pain. As a minister of hope, my answer is the same as it would be if the problem were in any other area. The message of the Christian church continues to be: Repentance and faith in Jesus Christ are still the answer for men and women falling short of the mark. Do not allow past failures to cause you to give up. Losing a battle doesn't mean the war is lost. We can't retrace our steps and we can't undo the past. We can, however, chart our course for the future. Do not excuse present behavior because of past failure. Confess your wrong and accept God's forgiveness.[10]

Dealing with Scars

Such action on your part does not mean that all the results of your sexual past will be eradicated. God forgives, but the natural results of our behaviors are not totally removed. A man who gets intoxicated and slams his car into a telephone pole, resulting in a broken arm and a demolished car, may have God's forgiveness before he goes to the hospital, but his arm is still broken and his car is lost. Thus, in our moral behavior, the scars of failure are not totally removed by confession. What, then, are we to do with these scars?

The biblical challenge is honesty in all things.[11] If we have been sexually active in the past and are now seriously thinking about marriage, we must be honest with our potential mate. Disclose fully what happened in your past. Marriage has no closets for skeletons. Your past is your past and can never be changed. Trust your partner to accept you as you are, not as he or she might wish you were. If such acceptance cannot be experienced, then marriage should not be consummated. You must enter marriage with all the cards on the table.

In addition to the acceptance of your potential mate, you must also accept yourself and overcome your own past. If, for example, you have a negative attitude toward sex because of past experiences, you must not sweep this under the rug and go on as though this attitude does not exist. Face it, and deal with it.

This may involve counseling and certainly involves the exploration of spiritual healing. For the Christian, this begins with an in-depth study of what the Scriptures say about our sexuality. One cannot come away from such a study without the impression that the biblical view of sexual intercourse within marriage is positive. It is wholesome, beautiful, and ordained of God. An understanding of the truth will liberate you from negative attitudes. Thank God for the truth and ask Him to change feelings to coincide with the truth. You are not destined to fail in marriage because of past failures. You will have roadblocks to overcome that would not be there if you had followed God's ideal. But He has come to heal our infirmities and to help us reach our potential.

In this section, I have been discussing foundations for marital unity. If sex is your only goal, then the matters discussed above may be relatively unimportant. If you only want someone to cook your meals or pay the rent, then all you need is a willing partner. If, on the other hand, your goal is total unity of life, then you ought to examine the foundation closely. If you find that the foundation is not strong enough to hold the weight of a lifetime commitment, then you should not marry.

One national study has found that 87 percent of never-married single adults said that they wanted to have one marriage that would last a lifetime.[12] They have seen the results of divorce in the lives of their parents, and that is not what they desire. Making a wise decision about whom you marry is the first step in having a lifelong, satisfying marriage.

THINGS TO THINK ABOUT

If you are involved in a dating relationship that has the potential of leading to marriage, the following questions will be a good starting point:

1. Are my partner and I on the same wavelength intellectually? (Do some of the exercises mentioned in this chapter: Read a newspaper or online news article and discuss its merits and implications; read a book and share your impressions with each other.)

2. To what degree have we surveyed the foundation of our social unity? (Explore the following areas: sports, music, dance, parties, and vocational aspirations.)

3. Do we have a clear understanding of each other's personality, strengths, and weaknesses? (Take a personality profile. This is normally done under the direction of a counselor who will interpret the information and help you discover potential areas of personality conflicts.)

4. To what degree have we excavated our spiritual foundations? (What are your beliefs about God, Scripture, organized religion, values, and morals?)

5. Are we being truthful with each other about our sexual histories? (Are you far enough along in the relationship to feel comfortable talking about this?) To what degree are you discussing your opinions about sexuality?

6. Have we discovered and are we speaking each other's primary love language? (It is in the context of a full love tank that we are most capable of honestly exploring the foundations of our relationship.)

12

they're not just for romantic relationships:

ROOMMATES, CLASSMATES, AND COWORKERS

LIVING IN THE FRESHMAN dorm was not one of the things Reed had anticipated about college life. He was used to having his own room. The thought of living with someone else was not a pleasant one. Reed was organized and disciplined. His greatest fear was having a roommate like his younger brother—messy and undisciplined.

Two months into freshman year, Reed's old fears were his new reality. His roommate, Brad, was a "party animal." His desk looked like a trash heap, his bunk was never made, and his dirty clothes were everywhere.

Reed was not a confrontational person, so he didn't say anything to Brad, but inside he was seething. I had known Reed for several years, so when I saw him one weekend I unwittingly asked, "How's college?"

" . . . ABOUT TO DRIVE ME CRAZY."

"College is fine," he said, "but my roommate is about to drive me crazy."

"How's that?" I asked. Reed proceeded to share his dilemma, concluding, "It's so bad I've actually thought about moving back home and commuting to college. But Mom and Dad don't want me to do that.

"I like Brad as a person, but I just can't stand his clutter. Do you have any ideas?"

Reed was desperate, so I said, "As a matter of fact, I do."

I began with the obvious: "As you know, we can't make other people change. But we can influence people to make changes.

"The greatest way to have a positive influence on anyone is to love them. You remember our class on *The Five Love Languages*, right?"

"Oh yeah," he said. "It helped me a ton in my dating relationships. But this isn't a romantic relationship."

"I understand," I said, smiling, "but it is a human relationship. And all humans need to feel loved. If you are going to request that someone make a change in their behavior, you are more likely to see that change if the person feels loved and appreciated by you."

I asked Reed if he knew Brad's primary love language. He was unsure, so I wrote all five on a sheet of paper and handed it to him. Then I asked whether he knew which of those love languages Brad expressed most often to others.

Reed's eyes ran down the list, and he quickly ruled out acts of service and physical touch.

Then he said, "I think it is words of affirmation. He's always thanking me for little things. He's a very positive person."

"Do you ever hear him complain about anything?"

Reed reflected for a moment and said, "Well, last week he was talking about his dad and said, 'I wish my dad could be more positive about life. He's always putting my mom down, and I don't like that. He doesn't realize how his words hurt her.'"

"And obviously hurt him," I added. "I think you are right. I think Brad's love language is words of affirmation. So if you want him to feel loved and appreciated, you've got to give him words of affirmation before you request behavior changes."

"But what can I affirm him for?" he said. "That's what bugs me. He's so sloppy."

"Let's look at other areas of his life," I suggested. "If you had to say something positive about Brad, what would you say?"

"Well, he's outgoing; he's friendly; and like I said, he's positive. He loaned me a few quarters the other night when I was getting ready to do my laundry. I don't know. There are some positive things about him. I just have a hard time seeing them with his dirty clothes all over the room."

"I WISH . . ."

"Let's focus on that a moment," I said. "What specific changes would you like to see Brad make?"

"I would like to see him keep his dirty socks off my chair."

"Let's write these down," I said, handing Reed a pen. "You make a list, and I'll make a list. What else would you like to see changed?"

"I wish he would put his dirty clothes in a laundry bag in the closet. I wish he would put his empty Coke cans in the garbage. I wish he would put his candy wrappers in the trash also. The other day, I found a Snickers bar on his desk, half eaten, covered with ants.

"I wish he would put his books on his desk, not on my desk. His desk is so cluttered he doesn't have room for his books."

I could tell that all of this was extremely irritating to Reed. "Anything else?" I asked.

"That's enough for now," he said. "And one other thing: I wish he would keep his shoes under the bed or in the closet, not in the middle of the floor."

"These seem like reasonable expectations to me," I said. "Now I'm going to give you a strategy for seeing these changes take place. For the next three weeks, don't mention any of them."

"Oh, I haven't mentioned them," said Reed, "except I did mention the ant invasion."

"Okay," I said. "If you want a person to change behavior, ultimately you have to tell him what you would like to see changed. People cannot read our minds. They don't know automatically what irritates us. However, that is not the place to start. For the next three weeks, I want you to concentrate on the positive things you can say about Brad."

MAKE A STRATEGY FOR CHANGE

"Set yourself a goal to make one affirming statement to him every day for the next three weeks. If his primary love language is words of affirmation, at the end of three weeks he will begin to feel loved and appreciated by you. Then you can make one request. Choose one from the list you made and simply say, 'Brad, I'd like to make one request of you. If it's possible, could you put your shoes under the bed or in the closet? I find myself tripping over them when you leave them in the middle of the room.'

"Then you say to him, 'By the way, if there is anything I'm doing that bothers you that you would like to see me change, I'd certainly be willing to change. I want us to have a good working relationship.' If Brad makes a suggestion, then to the best of your ability, make the change.

"After this first encounter, you continue to give affirming words at least three times a week, and every second week you make an additional request until you have exhausted your list. And each week you also open yourself up to the possibility of making a change. If this doesn't work, then you have my permission to put in for a roommate change second semester. If a person is going to change, they are most likely to do so when they feel loved and accepted by the person requesting the change."

Reed was not overly optimistic. But he said, "It makes a lot of sense, and I will certainly give it a try." I knew he was the kind of person who would be conscientious in following the plan we had mapped out.

I didn't see Reed again until Christmas break. I repeated my original question: "How's college?"

A smile broke on his face as he said, "You are amazing."

"Why do you say that?" I asked.

"I never believed when I sat in your office that afternoon that what you were saying would really work. But Brad and I are developing a real friendship. His shoes are under his bed, his dirty clothes are usually in the laundry bag, and his Coke cans are in the trash. Actually, he's found a recycling bin down the hallway, and he's all about that now."

"So what changes did he request of you?" I asked.

"The biggest one was that I would get a more focused lamp for my desk so that when I study after midnight, the big light won't keep him awake."

"Any other requests?" I probed.

Reed smiled. "Well, he did ask that I stop hugging his girlfriend every time I saw her. I didn't mean anything by it. I'm a hugger, but it irritated him. So, I backed off."

"And the rest of college is going well?" I asked.

"It's great," he said. "I love college."

"I'm glad," I said, "but one correction. I'm not amazing, love is amazing." We both smiled and hugged each other.

It's important to understand that this strategy was not an attempt for Reed to manipulate Brad. Manipulation is the use of fear or threat to force someone to do something against his will. Love is an effort to do something for the benefit of the other person, and sometimes this might be followed by a request to make life better for you.

Requests and demands are very different. Love creates the climate in which requests are more likely to be honored. Responding to a sincere request is also an expression of love. It is doing something for the benefit of the person making the request. Reciprocal love is the fabric of lasting friendships.

STRONGER BONDS, STRONGER FRIENDSHIPS

Friendships are cultivated and strengthened when we choose to speak each other's primary love language. Molly and Krista had known each other since the eighth grade. In high school they were both very involved with cheerleading. They never missed a game. The girls made scores of trips on athletic teams' buses with their pom-poms. During their senior year, each of them dated a football player. Krista dated Randy, the quarterback, and Molly dated Joe, a running back. It was a year filled with activities and excitement.

Unfortunately, it was also a year that ended in tragedy. Eight days before graduation, Joe was killed in an alcohol-related car accident. Graduation exercises continued as planned, but for Molly, it was a day of overwhelming grief.

Molly's Grief

Krista and Molly spent many hours together that summer. Krista accompanied Molly to a grief class taught in their church. She discovered the value of listening to Molly relive her experiences and conversations with Joe. Molly recalled many of her aspirations and eventually she came to terms with her comments to Joe about his drinking. "If only he had listened," Molly said.

Krista listened empathetically and occasionally asked questions. She was quickly learning that grief is often best processed through talking things out. When Molly's grief was accompanied with sobs of pain, Krista embraced her, and they cried together. The summer was filled with crying and conversation.

Though Molly had planned to go to college, she did not feel she was emotionally ready, so she took a job in her hometown and said good-bye to her friend Krista. Krista hated to leave her friend, but she knew that life had to go on. And for her, that meant college. Probably because of her experiences that summer and her concern for Molly, she took an elective class on human relationships at the university.

Krista's Insight

In her human relationships class, she was exposed to *The Five Love Languages* and realized almost immediately that Molly's primary love language was quality time and her secondary love language was physical touch. Without realizing it, she had been speaking Molly's love languages all summer.

This gave her a feeling of deep satisfaction. It also gave her the insight for which she had prayed: "How can I best help Molly through this crisis?" She knew now how to effectively help Molly. She committed herself to going home every other weekend and spending quality time with her friend. After a few weeks, she invited Molly to visit her on campus any weekend she desired. It was a semester of healing for Molly, and by January she was enrolled at the university. She was ready to move on with her life, deeply grateful for a friend who loved her.

The college years came and went. Krista married Randy. Molly married a young man she met at school. The two women moved to separate cities and pursued their dreams. Molly and Krista would call each other every three to four months just to check in and make sure things were going well. The years went much faster than either of them anticipated.

Once a year, they tried to spend a weekend together back in their hometown. Things seemed to be going fine until one summer on one of those weekend visits, Krista told Molly that she was afraid Randy was having an affair. Fears turned to reality, and within six months, Randy had left Krista. She was devastated.

Remembering Krista's help years earlier, Molly asked herself and her husband, Seth, "What can I do to help Krista?" She knew Krista's love language: acts of service. They had talked about it many times, and Krista complained often that Randy "never helps me around the house." She and Seth talked and agreed that if Krista were open to it, they would invite her to their city, "find her a place to live, help her get a job, and help her process the pain of rejection." They offered and Krista responded positively. They loved her through grief and back to health. Friends are always there for friends (not just when it's easy). And friends who understand the five love languages know how to be there most effectively.

REALLY CONNECT, REALLY SERVE

It seems as if the more technology we get, the more friends we have. The more we network on the Internet, the more we communicate over long distances, and the more we are able to multitask at everything—the bigger our circles become.

If we're not careful, this might result in a growing number of acquaintances, and a decreasing number of real, authentic friendships. However, we live in a brave new world and it might very well be out of this pool of acquaintances that those great friendships we all crave are born. Learning to use your own primary love language as a means of encouraging and loving others allows you to contribute meaningfully to the lives of the people around you.

Marcie, a young single adult, acknowledges that her love language is acts of service. "I receive the greatest joy by serving others," she said. "Professionally, I work in the food service industry. So, I volunteer to work in the kitchen at my church. We serve Wednesday night meals, and on special occasions we do banquets. One of the things I enjoy most is putting on a Valentine's banquet for the married couples at our church.

"It's commonly said that single people are always wanting," Marcie added, "but I believe that singles should be giving. This is my way of giving to others."

One of my personal joys through the years has been to encounter people who have the same philosophy as Marcie. Kelly's sister was a financially strapped single mother. She gave all her effort and resources to provide for her children, but no one was providing for her. So, when Kelly saw the opportunity, she offered to buy her sister a few new pairs of shoes and a couple new dresses.

At first her sister was reluctant, but when Kelly said, "I love you. And I want to help you," tears came to her sister's eyes, and she said, "I appreciate that." Gifts may not be her sister's primary love language, but when a person is in real need, gifts given in love, communicate love. Remember, even though we each have a primary language, we can still receive love in all five languages.

LOVE AT WORK TOO (YOU SPEND A LOT OF TIME WITH THESE PEOPLE)

Speaking someone's primary love language at work can build friendships and create a positive atmosphere in an environment that is often stressful. Coworkers appreciate having someone take the time to speak their particular love language.

A Hard Time: Speaking Cathy's Language

Susan developed a friendship with her nineteen-year-old coworker, Cathy, and soon discovered that Cathy's love language was gifts. So periodically, she would give Cathy some small token of appreciation. A few months later Cathy's boyfriend proposed, and while Susan questioned whether she was old enough to marry, she wasn't condemning.

Later on, when her fiancé broke off the engagement, Cathy was absolutely devastated.

Knowing Cathy's primary love language was gifts, "I made her a basket of treats," Susan recalled. "I included a book I knew she would like, some candy, and a card.

"The look on her face when she opened the basket was easily worth a million dollars. To be able to do something like that makes me feel good too."

What could be more important in life than giving and receiving love? Friendships are fostered by meaningful expressions of love, especially when such great thought goes into loving them in their own language.

A Difficult Situation: Showing Love to Becky

Speaking someone's love language on the job can even transform your attitudes toward a fellow worker. Lauren had a coworker whom she resented. Lauren felt that Becky didn't carry her part of the load. She wanted to have a better relationship, but she wasn't sure if it was possible. When she heard about the five love languages, the first person that came to mind was Becky.

"I wasn't sure what would happen," Lauren said, "but I knew I had to give it a chance. My first job was to discover Becky's primary love language. Since we didn't talk much, mainly because of my resentment, I wasn't sure how to proceed.

"I remembered something from Bible study a few weeks earlier. Jesus said, 'Love your enemies and pray for those who persecute you.'[1] I didn't feel like Becky was my enemy, and I didn't exactly sense that she was persecuting me, though I did feel she wasn't treating me fairly. So I prayed for her. Before long, I found myself praying that God would express His love to Becky through me.

"But I still didn't know her primary love language. I thought that if I gave her a gift, she might think that I was trying to 'buy her friendship.' In this situation, speaking the wrong love language could cause more harm than good. So I asked God to help me figure it out."

A New Year's Resolution

"It was the week after Christmas when I prayed this prayer. One morning I woke up, and while I was getting ready for work, this idea came to mind: *Why don't I make a New Year's resolution that within the first three months of the New Year I would do one thing for each person at work to make his or her life easier?* Obviously, the only way I could do that would be to tell them about my resolution and ask what I could do to make their life easier. I figured this might be a way to discover each of their love languages. And it worked," she said.

Lauren asked two other coworkers first, then Becky. She explained her New Year's resolution: "Do one thing for each person in the office that would make his or her life easier. So I'm asking you to think about it and, maybe tomorrow, give me an answer."

"Are you crazy?" Becky said. "You want to make my life easier?" Becky asked with what seemed to be a measure of hostility and disbelief.

"I may very well be crazy," Lauren responded, "but that's what I want to do."

"Okay," Becky said. "I'll think about it."

The next day when Lauren went back for her answer, she found Becky in a different mood. "I've been thinking about this," Becky said, "and the only way I'm going to do this is if it's a two-way street. It's not fair for you to do something for me unless I do something for you. So, if you'll tell me something I could do to make your life easier, then I'll answer your question."

Lauren was not ready for this response, and she said so: "Wow, I wasn't ready for that. Maybe you'd better give me a day to think about it, and I'll get back with you tomorrow."

That night, Lauren thought about what had happened. So far, she was just attempting to express love, and Becky was already reciprocating. Lauren knew that her own primary love language was acts of service. That's why she had been so irritated that Becky was not "carrying her load." But what could she ask Becky to do that would make her life easier? There were so many things she thought Becky should be doing, but she had to choose one, and she wanted to be honest and make it something that would genuinely be helpful to her. It was not until the next morning as Lauren drove to work that she decided on her request.

For the past three years, Lauren had been making coffee every morning. She wasn't sure how she acquired the job, but no one else ever offered to help. She knew it would be too much to ask Becky to take over that responsibility, but, she thought: *Perhaps she would be willing to do it one week and let me do it the next week. We could take turns, and it wouldn't be a burden on either one of us.* It seemed doable and something that would be genuinely meaningful to her.

That morning, over a proverbial cup of coffee, Becky said, "You go first."

"Wait a minute," Lauren said. "I initiated this. I think you should go first."

"I know you initiated it," said Becky, laughing. "That's why I think you ought to go first. Besides, it's going to be hard for me to share mine, but if I can hear yours first, then I promise, I'll share it."

"Okay," said Lauren, "what we're sharing is something the other person could do that would make our life easier, right?"

"Right," said Becky.

"Well, as you know, I make the coffee every morning. I really don't know how I got the job. I don't really mind it, but I thought if you could make the coffee one week and I make it the next week, we could take turns. It would certainly make my life easier, and maybe it wouldn't be too hard on either one of us. Well, what do you think?" asked Lauren.

Becky answered thoughtfully, "I could do that. I never thought about it. I guess I just assumed that was part of your job."

"Well, it all started three years ago," Lauren said, "when John bought the coffeepot. Before that we just used instant coffee. I volunteered the first week, and after that, it was just my job."

"I'd be happy to do that," said Becky. "You want me to start this week?"

"No, I'll finish this week," said Lauren. "You can start next week. Now, it's your turn."

Surprise! Different People Respond Differently

"Mine's very different," she said. "It may sound crazy . . . I've been working here for four years. I think I do a pretty good job, though I know sometimes I'm a little slow at getting new things. But I don't ever feel much appreciation. I feel like my work is just taken for granted.

"So what I'd like to ask is . . . " She paused. "This is really hard," she said. "I feel so silly saying this. I guess what I'm asking is if once in a while you see me doing a good job, could you just tell me? Positive words have always meant a lot to me. I feel like all I ever get is criticisms, not so much from you, but I would just like to feel that somebody thinks I'm doing a good job."

Lauren was having a hard time processing what she was hearing, but she knew this was Becky's primary love language.

"I think everybody likes to hear words of appreciation from time to time," Lauren said. "And I can certainly do that."

"See," said Becky. "I told you mine was different."

"That's all right," said Lauren. "One of the things I've been learning is that what makes one person feel loved and appreciated doesn't necessarily make another person feel appreciated. For me, it's when people do things for me. For you it's when people express appreciation for what you've done. So, let's try this and see if it works."

Lauren went back to work knowing this was the most in-depth conversation she had ever had with Becky and knowing also that Becky had opened a window into her emotional love tank. That night, Lauren prayed that God would help her see the positive things Becky did and help her express sincere verbal appreciation. (Part 2 of this story is coming . . . in chapter 14.)

SPEAKING LOVE TO FRIENDS WITH SPECIFIC NEEDS

Debra has a single parent friend whose primary love language is words of affirmation and whose secondary language is quality time. Last year, Debra started one week before her birthday and sent her a card every day of that week. She ended the week by taking her out to dinner. Knowing her friend's primary love language allowed Debra to speak love more deeply and more effectively than if she had just blindly guessed what would make her feel loved.

Paula is a caregiver for Shannon, a young girl with cerebral palsy.

"I knew that I could help her physically, but I kept asking, 'How can I communicate emotional love to this child?' I know children need to feel loved. Then I heard about the five love languages, so I began observing Shannon's behavior. I began to notice how Shannon responded to me when I spoke each of the five love languages.

"She responded most positively when I gave her tender touches or words of affirmation. I also noticed that the two languages she reciprocated were touch and words of affirmation. Every day when I arrived, she would give me a big hug, and the performance was repeated when I got ready to leave. Every day she told me several times, 'I love you.'

"Since words are my primary love language, I certainly feel loved by Shannon, and I believe she senses my love very deeply."

Paula discovered that even children and adults who have physical or mental challenges respond positively to expressions of emotional love, especially when the time is taken to learn their primary love language.

Most single adults would like to have growing relationships with roommates, classmates, coworkers, and the other significant people in their lives. Love in any language enhances relationships. But love spoken in one's primary love language communicates on an even deeper emotional level.

THINGS TO THINK ABOUT

1. Do you have a significant relationship with any of your high school classmates? If so, list their names and answer the following question: What might I do to discover this person's primary love language? If you believe you already know their primary love language, ask: How might I speak their love language this week?

2. If you are attending or have attended college, how would you describe the friendships you developed with classmates? If you are finished with school, have you maintained a friendship with any of your classmates? What steps might you take to deepen these relationships?

3. If you are employed, list the names of the people you work with most often. Do you know the primary love language of these people? What might you do to discover it?

4. With whom would you like to have a better working relationship? What steps will you take?

5. In addition to parents and siblings, who are the other significant people in your life? What is the most recent expression of love you have given these individuals?

6. Do you know the primary love language of each of these significant people? What steps might you take to discover and/or speak their love language?

13

single with kids:
LOVE LANGUAGES AND
SINGLE PARENTS

ANGIE IS A SINGLE MOM with two teenagers, Josh, fifteen, and Julie, thirteen. Her world is not easy. It hasn't been easy for a long time. Her husband left when the children were eight and ten. After going through the trauma of a difficult divorce and working through her own sense of rejection, Angie took charge of her life.[1]

With her parents' help, she finished her nurse's training and since then has worked at the local hospital. She wouldn't have made it financially without working full-time because her husband's child support payments were inadequate and often sporadic.

In spite of all her accomplishments, Angie lives with an underlying sense of guilt. She has been unable to spend as much time with the children as she would like. Because of her job, she has missed many of their after-school activities. Now they are teenagers, and she still can't spend as much time with them as she would like.

They are growing up and changing, and she wonders if they are ready for what lies ahead. One day she tells herself, *I did the best I could*. The next day she says, *I'm not sure I did enough.* Lately, Josh has been talking back and often criticizes his mom. Julie wants to start dating, and Angie thinks she is too young.

In my office one day, Angie said, "I'm not sure I am up to this. I think I've done fairly well up until now, but I don't know if I can endure the teenage years." Angie was saying the same things I have heard from hundreds of single parents through the years. "Will someone please help me? I'm not sure I can do this by myself."

A near certain reality in our nonstop world is sometimes feeling overwhelmed or alone. My hope for this book and its message is to encourage and help the thousands of single parents like Angie. Perhaps you are a single parent or you know a single parent who could use some encouragement and help. Either way, discovering the primary love language of your child will help you invest the time you *do* have in the best possible way to meet the emotional needs of your child. Both the primary caregivers and the lesser-involved parents will be more effective in loving their children if they regularly speak the child's primary love language and sprinkle in the other four when they have the opportunity. Children need to experience all five of the love languages, but without their primary love language, their emotional love tank will likely remain empty.

Kevin had just spent the weekend with his son, Matt. They watched football, washed the car, and played two games of miniature golf. Kevin felt good about their time together. He would have been shocked had he heard Matt's comments to his counselor the following Tuesday afternoon. When asked, "How did the weekend go with your father?" Matt responded, "We did a lot of things together. But I don't think my father loves me."

"Why do you say that?" the counselor asked.

"Because he never talks to me about what I'm thinking and feeling."

It is not uncommon that fathers and children have different views about their visitation relationship. Research indicates that the father often thinks he has been loving and attentive, but the child still feels rejected. One study indicated that while most fathers thought they had fulfilled their obligations, three out of four teenagers had the impression that they did not mean much to their fathers.[2]

This same difference of perception may also be true between the child and the parent who is the primary caregiver. Ten-year-old Tyler said, "My mother works hard. I guess she loves me, but I wish she wouldn't criticize me so much."

Helping Your Child Feel Loved . . .

The question is not: "Do you as a single parent love your children?" The question is: "Do your children feel loved?" Parental sincerity is not enough. We must learn to speak the child's primary love language. I am convinced that much of the misbehavior of children is rooted in an empty love tank. Each child has a primary love language—the language that speaks most deeply to his soul and meets his emotional need to feel loved. If parents fail to discover and speak the child's primary love language, then he may feel unloved even though the parent is speaking other languages.

Let me briefly review the five love languages, and let's focus on seeking to apply them to your child.

. . . Through Words of Affirmation

This language lets you affirm your child's worth through verbal expression. "I love you. You look nice in that dress. You did a good job making your bed. Great catch! Thanks for helping me wash the car. I'm proud of you." These are words of affirmation.

The simple words "I love you" can be like gentle rain falling on the soul of the child. In contrast, harsh or cutting words, spoken out of anger, can damage a child's self-esteem and be remembered for a lifetime.

Ten-year-old Tyler demonstrated that words of affirmation was his primary love language when he said, "I guess she loves me, but I wish she wouldn't criticize me so much." Tyler was also demonstrating another reality—that when you use a child's primary love language in a negative way, it hurts that child more deeply than it would hurt another child. Since Tyler's primary love language was words of affirmation, his mother's negative words cut more deeply into his heart.

... Through Gifts

A gift says, "Someone was thinking about me. Look what they got for me." Gifts need not be expensive. They can be as simple as a stone you picked up walking down the street or a flower you picked in the front yard. To make the most of gifts as an expression of love, wrap them up and present them. Even school clothes offered this way can become gifts from a single parent.

A gift is never given because a child made his bed or cleaned his room. Such a gift is payment for services rendered, not a true gift at all. Gifts are given because the single parent loves, not because a child deserves.

If you return from a trip and bring your two daughters a teddy bear, don't be surprised if one jumps up and down and says, "Thank you, thank you," gives the teddy bear a name, and places it in a special place in her room, while the other one says, "Thank you," tosses her bear on the couch, and starts asking you about your trip. The second daughter is demonstrating her primary love language: quality time. She is more interested in your attention than in your gift, while the first child definitely has the primary love language of gifts.

... Through Acts of Service

Doing things for a child that the child cannot do for himself is an expression of love. We speak this language early by changing diapers, feeding, and responding to the infant's physical needs. Over the next eighteen years, life is filled with preparing meals, washing clothes, putting on Band-Aids, repairing bicycles, and a thousand other acts of service. If done in a spirit of kindness, these are emotional expressions of love.

As children get older, we serve them by teaching them the skills necessary to take care of themselves: cooking meals gives way to teaching them to prepare meals.

Acts of service are a powerful way of communicating emotional love to children. Mandy, age ten, said, "I know my mother loves me because she helps me with my homework, especially my math."

... Through Quality Time

Quality time is giving your child your undivided attention. With a small child, it is sitting on the floor, rolling a ball back and forth, or sitting on the couch while reading a book. With an older child, it may be taking a walk through the woods, where the two of you look, listen, and talk. Because children are at different levels of maturation, if we are to spend quality time with them, we must go where they are. We must discover their interests and enter into their worlds.

Physical proximity does *not* equal quality time. A father and a son watching a football game is quality time only if the child senses that he is the focus of his father's attention. If the father's attention is on the game, the son may feel rejected, as Matt demonstrated earlier. He and his father did activities together, but Matt came away emotionally empty, "because he never talks to me about what I'm thinking and feeling."

... Through Physical Touch

Physical touch includes hugs and kisses, but it also involves a pat on the back, a hand on the shoulder, holding hands as you cross the street, or even wrestling on the floor.

I asked eleven-year-old Jason, "On a scale of zero to ten, how much does your father love you?"

Without blinking an eye, he answered, "Ten!"

When I asked why he felt so strongly, he said, "Dad is always bumping me when he walks by, and we wrestle on the floor."

Remember, physical touch is a powerful communicator of emotional love.

RESPECT EACH CHILD'S UNIQUE LOVE LANGUAGE

Perhaps you are thinking, *Okay, I do some of those. So my child feels loved, right?* Not necessarily. Just as one form of discipline does not work with all children, so one love language does not work with all children. Each child has a primary love language that speaks to him or her more deeply than the other four. The love language of that child may be different than the language in which their sibling hears love. If we are to be successful in meeting our child's need for love, we must discover each child's primary love language and speak it regularly. This is the most effective way of keeping your child's love tank full.

I'm not suggesting that you only speak your son or daughter's primary love language. They need all five, but he/she needs heavy doses of his or her primary love language.

A single dad said, "I have twin daughters who are now four years old. My wife and I divorced about a year ago. I must confess I knew little about how to relate to my daughters. Now that they are getting a little older, I knew that I had to improve my fathering abilities. Someone gave me the book *The Five Love Languages of Children* and I read it. I was amazed to learn that my twin daughters had such different love languages. One is physical touch and the other is quality time. Now that I'm learning to speak their primary love language, I am sensing a much closer bond between us."

HOW TO DISCOVER YOUR CHILD'S LOVE LANGUAGE

So how do you discover your child's primary love language? Let's review the principles we talked about earlier:

1. *Observe how your child expresses love to you.* If your daughter is always looking for a hug, this may be an indication that her primary love language is physical touch. If your son is always giving praise or thanks—"Mommy, this is a good meal"—his love language may be words of affirmation.

2. *Listen to your child's requests.* What the child requests most often is a clue to his/her primary love language. "Daddy, can we go to the park?" "Mommy, can you read me a story?" These children are asking for quality time, and it is probably their primary love language.

3. *Listen to the complaints.* "Why didn't you bring me a present?" may be your son's way of telling you that his love language is gifts. "We don't ever go to the beach anymore since Daddy left" may be an indication that the child's primary love language is quality time.

If these three approaches do not reveal your child's primary language, then you can experiment by focusing on speaking one of the five love languages each week and observing your child's response. When you are speaking his primary love language, you will see a noticeable difference in his attitude toward you.

Kathi described herself as "a struggling single mom who desperately wants to raise my children in the context of a loving relationship." After her divorce, she had several problems with her children. In a search to understand how to respond, she read *The Five Love Languages of Children*. There she recognized her kids' different love languages.

"I discovered that receiving gifts was my oldest child's primary love language. Miranda blossomed as I gave her little gifts. Not expensive things; just little tokens of love. She brags to people and tells them what I gave her. It has changed her attitude toward me.

"My son, Jordan, who is now ten, has the love language of quality time. He loves for me to spend time with him. We read books together at night, and I have learned to enjoy watching him play video games. He just likes me there watching him play. My full attention is sometimes hard to get, but when I set aside time just for Jordan, he thrives on it."

Let me encourage you not only to speak the primary love language of your child but also to inform grandparents, aunts, uncles, and other significant adults of the primary love language of your child. Children need to receive love from extended family and friends as well their primary caregivers.

DISCIPLINE AND THE LOVE LANGUAGES

Patti attended one of my workshops for single parents and realized immediately that words of affirmation was her eleven-year-old Phillip's primary love language. She also knew that in the last six weeks, she had given Phillip a lot of negative words about his schoolwork and the way he treated his sister. She determined that over the next few weeks she would give him a positive statement of affirmation every day.

"I couldn't believe what happened," Patti said. "In less than a week, Phillip had a whole different countenance. He started doing his homework first thing every afternoon, even without my prodding. And I saw noticeable change in his attitude and treatment of his sister. It's hard to believe that simply speaking his primary love language would make such a difference."

Keep the Love Tank Full

Keeping a child's love tank full will not eliminate all misbehavior. But it does mean that a child is less likely to misbehave if the love tank is full.

When your child does misbehave and discipline is necessary, parents will profit by making sure the love tank is full before giving the discipline. The child who receives discipline while the love tank is empty will almost certainly rebel against the discipline.

Express Love Before and After the Discipline

Therefore, I encourage single parents before administering discipline to consciously speak the love language of your child. Then after the discipline, give your son or daughter an additional expression of love.

For example, let's assume you have a rule that the football is not to be thrown inside the house, and the consequence for breaking the rule is that the football will go in the trunk of the car for two days. In addition, if anything is broken, the child will pay for the broken object out of his or her allowance. So, what happens when your child breaks the rule? You both already know the discipline, but how you administer it is extremely important. Let's assume that the child's love language is words of affirmation. You might administer the discipline in the following manner.

You walk into the room and say to him, "One of the things I really appreciate about you is that you almost always keep the rules. To me, that's a very positive trait and a sign of genuine maturity. I really appreciate that about you. However, as you know, you threw the football in the house, and a glass was broken. Therefore, we both know that the ball has to go into the trunk of the car, and you'll have to pay for the glass out of your allowance. But what makes me so proud of you is that this happens so seldom, and I am really glad about that."

You have wrapped the discipline in love, and your child will likely receive it in a positive manner.

If, on the other hand, you walk into the room and simply say, "You know you are not supposed to throw the football in the house. Now, look at what you've done. You've broken a glass. You know the results of this. Go put the football into the trunk of the car, and your allowance this week will have to go to buying the glass." And then you walk out of the room.

Your child will likely put the ball into the trunk of the car while saying to himself, *I try to obey the rules. I mess up one time and she comes in screaming at me.*

A child rebels not against the discipline but against the manner in which the discipline is rendered. The child will feel rejected rather than loved.

MEET YOUR OWN NEED FOR LOVE

While I have talked primarily about meeting the child's need for love, I am keenly aware that the single parent is also a creature of need. In *The Five Love Languages of Children* I mention the need for single parents to address their own needs to love:

> While a child is working through the emotions of guilt, fear, anger, and insecurity, one or both parents are also working through similar emotions. The mother who has been abandoned by a husband may have [feelings of rejection and anger]; the mother who forced a physically abusive spouse to leave now struggles with her own feelings of

hurt and loneliness. A single parent's emotional need for love is just as real as anyone else's need. Because that need cannot be met by the former spouse or by the child, the single parent often reaches out to friends. This is an effective way to begin to have your love tank filled. . . .

[However], the single parent at this point is extremely vulnerable to members of the opposite sex who may take advantage in a time of weakness. Because the single parent so desperately needs love, there is grave danger in accepting that love from someone who will take advantage sexually, financially, or emotionally. It is extremely important that the newly single parent be very selective in making new friends. The safest source of love is from long-term friends or members of the extended family. A single parent who tries to satisfy the need for love in an irresponsible manner can end up with tragedy upon tragedy.[3]

If you have experienced divorce or death of a spouse, give yourself time to grieve and heal. As often as possible, talk to extended family and friends. Talking about your hurt, anger, frustration, and struggles is the fastest way to process grief. Take advantage of classes offered by local churches or community agencies that focus on single parents.

Working through your own struggles in a positive way is a powerful example for your children. Psychologists Sherill and Prudence Tippins have said, "The best gift you can give your child is your own emotional, physical, spiritual, and intellectual health."[4] As painful as it may seem to admit, the truth is that you may be a single parent for many years. During this time, long or short, you will want to give your children an example of integrity and responsibility that can be a model for them in their journey to responsible adulthood. Hopefully, understanding the five love languages will help you reach that objective.

THINGS TO THINK ABOUT

1. If you don't know your child's primary love language, try answering the following questions to help you figure it out:

   - How does my child most often express love to others?

   - What does he/she complain about most often?

   - What does my child request most often?

2. How might you improve your method of discipline by using your child's primary love language?

3. Make a list of the feelings your child has experienced because of a missing or distant parent: fear, anger, anxiety, denial, blame, etc. How can you use your child's primary love language to help alleviate the pain in each case?

4. As a single parent, how do you meet your own emotional need for love? Who are the significant people in your life (family or friends) to whom you could turn for emotional support? Perhaps you could begin by expressing appreciation to them for the role they have played in your life. Later make a specific request for their help.

5. Are you a part of a single parent class in your church or community? If not, whom could you contact to find out about such a class? If you cannot find such a class, perhaps you could start a class for single parents.[5]

14

success:

LOVE IS THE KEY

I'VE NEVER MET a single adult who aspired to become a failure. Everyone wants to succeed. But what is success? Ask a dozen people and you may get a dozen answers.

I once heard that when the late billionaire J. Paul Getty was asked that question, he responded, "Rise early, work late, and strike oil!" Perhaps that formula worked for Getty, but it is not likely to work for you. A friend of mine shared this definition: "Success is making the most of who you are with what you've got." I like that.

Every person has the potential to make a positive impact on the world. Success is not measured by the amount of money you possess or the position you attain but rather in what you do with what you've got. Position and money can be squandered or abused, but they can also be used to help others.

We typically speak of success in specific areas of life, such as financial success, educational success, or vocational success. We also attach the word to sports, family, religion, and relationships. What we mean when we say that people are successful in one of these areas is that they accomplished the goals they set for themselves.

Whatever the category and whatever our view of success, we are more likely to succeed if we effectively love people.

SUCCESS IN BUSINESS . . .

Let's think for a moment of business success. Tom Peters, author of *Thriving on Chaos*, said, "Only companies that stay attached to their customers will survive and prosper."[1] Peters is talking about relationships. True business success is always built on relationships.

Psychologist Kevin Leman, author of *Winning the Rat Race Without Becoming a Rat*, offers three laws for success in business:

> Number One: *People love to buy anything, especially if they like the person who is selling it to them.*
> Number Two: *You build relationships one conversation at a time.*
> Number Three: *Know your customers and selling your product will take care of itself.*[2]

Leman concludes that the Golden Rule, "Treat others as you would like to be treated," is the key to all successful businesses.[3] All of these business principles call for an attitude of love and will be greatly strengthened by knowing and speaking the primary love language of your business associates.

. . . AND SUCCESS IN RELATIONSHIPS

What is true as a guiding principle for business success is also true in the field of human resources. Many successful companies have realized that their greatest asset is the people who work for them. They also recognize that negative work environments can create a tension that rules the office, and productivity is decreased. I know of nothing more effective in changing the work climate than understanding and practicing the concepts of the five love languages.

BACK TO BECKY AND LAUREN

Do you remember Lauren, whom we met in chapter 12? She resented her coworker, Becky, because she felt like Becky was not carrying her part of the workload. Lauren decided to try to discover Becky's primary love language and see what would happen if she expressed meaningful love and appreciation to her. She did this by making a New Year's resolution that she wanted to do one thing for each of her coworkers that would make their lives easier. So she asked Becky and the others to give her a suggestion.

Becky turned the tables on Lauren and said, "I will if you will." After reflection, Lauren agreed. She requested that Becky help her by sharing the responsibility of making coffee each morning for the office staff. After Becky said yes, she asked Lauren to acknowledge when she did something well: "Positive words have always meant a lot to me, and I feel like all I ever get is criticisms. I would just like to feel that somebody thinks I'm doing a good job." It was obvious to Lauren that Becky's primary love language was words of affirmation. Here is the rest of the story:

Lauren struggled greatly with Becky's request. Remember, she felt resentment toward Becky for not carrying her part of the workload. How could she give her words of affirmation when she felt so resentful? Since Becky had agreed to help Lauren by making the coffee every other week, Lauren decided to start with that. On Wednesday of the first week, Lauren said to Becky, "I can't tell you how much I appreciate your making the coffee this week. It feels so great to have a break from that responsibility. I really appreciate you helping me with this."

"If There's Anything Else I Can Do . . ."

"I'm glad to help," Becky said. "I appreciate you giving me the opportunity to help you. If there is anything else I can do for you, please don't hesitate to ask."

Lauren walked back to her desk stunned. She couldn't believe what Becky had just said. After two years of resenting her for not carrying her part of the workload, Becky was now volunteering to help. *Why didn't I discover this love language concept sooner?* she said to herself. *But dare I ask her to do something else for me?* she mused. *Certainly I can't do that without giving her another compliment in some other area, but what could that be?*

Lauren pushed her thoughts aside and went back to work. The next day she noticed something different about Becky's hair. In the past, she wouldn't have mentioned it because of her resentment for Becky, but today she found herself freely saying, "I like how you're wearing your hair today. It's great."

"Thanks," said Becky. "I've been wanting to do something different for a long time. I finally got up the courage."

"Well, it really looks nice," said Lauren.

Two days later, Lauren found herself saying to Becky, "I noticed that you were still working when I left the office last night. Did you work very long?"

"About twenty minutes," Becky said. "I just wanted to finish the project I was on."

"I really appreciate that," said Lauren. "That's certainly going beyond the call of duty. I'm going to mention that to Ray just so he'll know how hard you've been working."

"Oh, wow, thanks," said Becky. "That'd be great."

Lauren sat down at her desk and thought, *I'm really getting into this thing.*

"I'd Be Happy to . . ."

The following week she went to Becky and said, "You know the other day when you mentioned that if I had something else you could help me with, you would be willing to do it?"

"Yes," said Becky.

"There is one thing. I know you said you were going down to the print shop later today. Could you get me some plain white printer paper while you're there?"

"I'd be happy to," said Becky.

"In fact," Lauren said, "we could even take turns with that like we do the coffeemaker, if you want. At least both of us won't be making the same trip every week."

"Oh, I'll be happy to do it," said Becky. "I like going to the print shop. There is a new guy down there that I've got my eye on. So far, he hasn't been very responsive, but I'm hoping."

They both laughed, and Lauren walked away.

Over the next few months, Lauren continued giving Becky words of affirmation, and Becky continued responding to Lauren's occasional request for help. Before the year was out, they found themselves going out for lunch together, something they had never done earlier.

"We actually became friends. It was hard to believe," Lauren said. "It demonstrated for me the power of love, especially when you are speaking someone's primary love language. I have to admit, it has changed the whole atmosphere, not only in my relationship with Becky but with the rest of our office staff."

Lauren loved her way to a successful relationship with Becky.

IS IT HYPOCRITICAL TO LOVE?

Act Like You Love the Person

Some may question the concept of loving someone you resent. Isn't that being hypocritical? You have negative feelings, but you are doing or saying something positive. When I hear that question, I am reminded of what the British scholar C. S. Lewis said:

> The rule for all of us is perfectly simple. Do not waste time bothering whether you "love" your neighbor; act as if you did. As soon as we do this, we find one of the great secrets. When you are behaving as if you love someone, you will presently come to love him. If you injure someone you dislike, you will find yourself disliking him more. If you do him a good turn, you will find yourself disliking him less.[4]

Your Feelings Aren't Always Right

Love is sometimes the choice to go against your feelings. It's similar to what I do every morning when I get up. I don't know about you, but if I only got out of bed on the mornings I felt like getting out of bed, I'd pretty much never get up. Almost every morning, including this morning, I go against my feelings, get up, do something I think to be good, and before the day is over, I feel good about having done it. *Love is not a feeling; it is a way of behaving.* Feelings follow behavior; therefore, loving feelings follow loving behavior. Loving actions on my part not only bring me positive feelings about myself, but, if spoken in the love language of the other person, they will stimulate positive feelings inside them.

Someone once said, "Following the path of least resistance is what makes people and rivers crooked. People seldom drift to success." Love takes effort, but the dividends are enormous.

ON THE ROAD TO SUCCESSFUL RELATIONSHIPS

Learning to discover and speak the love language of others is a giant step down the road of success.

Tim, an avid outdoorsman, made a choice to devote more time indoors to his elderly mother once he knew her love language. He asked her to share his house when he learned she was considering moving and possibly renting an apartment.

"Mom is now seventy-three years old and has many health problems. When I heard of the five love languages, I realized that my mother's love language is quality time. Thus, I started making time each day to sit down and talk with her. Before that, I simply assumed she would feel loved because I was providing for her. But I have seen a difference in her countenance since I've started giving her quality time.

"I want to continue to understand and apply the five love languages concept to my relationships with Mom, other family members, friends, and, maybe someday, a special relationship with a Christian woman." Tim has learned that love leads to success.

Evaluating Our Progress

Evaluation has become a key word in many companies. In fact, you may identify with Darcy, who said, "I'm feeling a little nervous today, because this afternoon I'm having my annual evaluation with my boss. I think things are okay, but you just never know."

The point of an evaluation is generally not to frighten the employee; the point is to focus on the purpose of the job and how well that purpose is being fulfilled. In short, an evaluation is to find out if you are succeeding. It is a practice that could yield positive fruit if applied to our relationships.

Years ago I heard a story about a young boy who walked into a drugstore and asked to use the telephone. He dialed a certain number and then said, "Hello, Dr. Anderson? Do you want to hire a boy to cut the grass and run errands for you?

"Oh, you already have someone who does that? Are you completely satisfied with his work? Okay then. Good-bye."

As the boy thanked the pharmacist, the pharmacist said, "Just a minute, Son. If you are looking for work, I could use a boy like you."

"Thank you, sir, but I have a job," the boy replied.

"But didn't I just hear you trying to get a job with Dr. Anderson?"

"No, sir," said the boy. "I'm the boy who is working for Dr. Anderson. I was just checking up on myself."

Perhaps we could all profit from checking up on ourselves. Imagine saying to a friend, coworker, or family member, "If I could make one change that would make life better for you, what would it be?" If you are bold enough to ask, then be strong enough to listen. What you hear will give you the information you need to improve your relationship with that person.

Perhaps you are saying, "But what if they request something that is extremely difficult for me to do?" My reply is, "That is what love is all about—doing something for the benefit of another!" If we do only what is easy, we will never succeed. There is one sure way of knowing you are on the right track towards success—the track is usually uphill.

Loving Those Who Don't Love Us

Most of us don't have a problem loving people who love us back. That is why the challenge Jesus gave His followers seems so unattainable: "You have heard that it was said, 'Love your neighbor and hate your enemy.' But I tell you: Love your enemies and pray for those who persecute you."[5]

It is interesting that Jesus gave God as our model when He said, "Your

Father in heaven . . . causes his sun to rise on the evil and the good, and sends rain on the righteous and the unrighteous."[6]

Perhaps you are thinking, *That's fine for God but I'm not God. I cannot love the people who have mistreated me in life.* Apart from God's help, that is true. But the Scriptures say, "God has poured out his love into our hearts by the Holy Spirit, whom he has given us."[7] Love is the central message of the Christian church. "God demonstrates his own love for us in this: While we were still sinners, Christ died for us."[8] Imagine what would happen if the single adults who call themselves Christians truly acted this way. Everyone desperately needs love. And those who give love are those who truly succeed.

Mother Teresa of Calcutta captured the truth well. When asked, "How do you measure the success of your work?" she looked puzzled for a moment and then replied, "I don't remember that the Lord ever spoke of success. He spoke only of faithfulness in love. This is the only success that really counts."[9] Mother Teresa left an indelible mark upon the world for one reason. She opened her heart to be a channel of God's love to others.

The greatest contribution any single adult can make is to become an effective channel of God's love. It is my prayer that this book will enable you to do that more effectively.

THINGS TO THINK ABOUT

1. What degree of success do you feel in your vocational relationships? If you wanted to improve relationships with your coworkers, with whom would you begin?

2. What question might you ask that would help you discover his/her primary love language? (Perhaps you will want to refer to the second half of chapter 8 in formulating such a question.) If you already know your coworker's primary love language, what might you say or do this week that would communicate love more effectively?

3. Is there a person in your life for whom you feel resentment? What happened to stimulate this emotion? What steps could you take to love your way to success in this relationship?

4. What is your most stressful relationship at the moment? Would you be willing to map out a strategy for improving this relationship by learning to speak that person's primary love language?

5. To what degree are you drawing upon the love of God in your efforts to love others? How might you strengthen your love relationship with God?[10]

NOTES

CHAPTER 1: *Single Adults*

1. "Facts for Features, Census Bureau Reports" U.S. Census Bureau, July 16, 2007, www.census.gov/Press-Release/www/releases/archives/ facts_for_features_special_editions/010329 .html.

2. George Barna, *Single Focus* (Ventura, Calif.: Regal, 2003), 8.

3. Ibid., 12.

4. Ruben G. Rumbaut and Glonaz Komaie, "Young Adults in the United States," research network working paper of The Network on Transitions to Adulthood, September 2007, www.transad.pop.upenn.edu/trends/index.html

5. National Center for Health Statistics, Vital Statistics of the United States, 2001 (Washington, D.C.), 42.

6. Centers for Disease Control and Prevention, First Marriage Dissolution, Divorce and Remarriage in the United States (Washington, D.C.), May 2001 Report.

7. Barna, *Single Focus*, 11. The National Center for Health Statistics reports that 75 percent of these divorced individuals eventually will remarry.

8. U.S. Bureau of the Census, Statistical Abstract of the United States, 2000 (Washington, D.C.), Table 55.

9. The U.S. Census Bureau reports that 12.9 million single parents are living with their children; see "Facts for Features," www.census.gov/Press-Release/www/releases/archives/ facts_for_features_special_editions/010329.html

10. Barna, *Single Focus*, 16.

11. Leo Buscaglia, *Love* (New York: Fawcett Crest, 1972), 55–56.

CHAPTER 2: *This Is It*

1. Dorothy Tennov, *Love and Limerence* (New York: Stein and Day, 1972), 142.

CHAPTER 3: *Love Language #1*

1. Proverbs 18:21. NLV   6. Proverbs 16:24

2. Luke 6:38.   7. Proverbs 10:11

3. 1 John 4:19 (NKJV).   8. " " 15:4

4. Proverbs 15:1.   9. " " 10:31

5. Proverbs 6:17

CHAPTER 4: *Love Language #2*

1. Gary Chapman, *The Five Love Languages* (Chicago: Northfield, 1992), 75.

CHAPTER 5: *Love Language #3*

1. Philip Yancey, *Leadership*, Fall 1995, 41.

2. See John 13:3–17.

3. Galatians 5:13.

4. Acts 20:35.

5. As quoted in Leo Buscaglia, *Love* (New York: Fawcett Crest, 1972), 58.

CHAPTER 6: *Love Language #4*

1. As quoted in Leo Buscaglia, *Love* (New York: Fawcett Crest, 1972), 17.

2. Buscaglia, *Love*, 77.

CHAPTER 7: *Love Language #5*

1. Leo Buscaglia, *Love* (New York: Fawcett Crest, 1972), 104.

2. Kersti Yllo and Murray A. Straus, "Interpersonal Violence among Married and Cohabiting Couples," Family Relations 30 (1981): 343.

3. Erich Fromm, *The Art of Loving* (New York: Harper & Row, 1956), 77–78.

4. Pitirim A. Sorokin, *The American Sex Revolution* (Boston: Porter Sargent, 1956), 3.

5. Glenn T. Stanton, *Why Marriage Matters* (Colorado Springs: Pinon, 1997), 53.

6. William G. Axinn and Arland Thornton, "The Relationship between Cohabitation and Divorce: Selectivity or Causal Influence?" *Demography* 29 (1992): 357–74.

7. Jan E. Stets, "The Link between Past and Present Intimate Relationships," *Journal of Family Issues* 14 (1993): 236–260.

8. Edward Laumann, John Gagnon, Robert Michael, and Stuart Michaels, *Social Organization of Sexuality: Sexual Practices in the United States* (Chicago: Univ. of Chicago Press, 1994), Table 11.12.

9. Linda G. Waite and Maggie Gallagher, *The Case for Marriage* (New York: Doubleday, 2000), 91.

10. Gary Chapman, *The Five Love Languages of Teenagers* (Chicago: Northfield, 2005), 67.

Chapter 9: *Family*

1. Exodus 20:12.

2. Ephesians 6:2–3.

Chapter 10: *Dating Relationships — Part 1*

1. Erich Fromm, *The Art of Loving* (New York: Harper & Row, 1956), 1–2.

2. James 1:19.

3. Matthew 20:28.

4. Matthew 20:26.

Chapter 11: *Dating Relationships — Part 2*

1. Linda J. Waite and Maggie Gallagher, *The Case for Marriage: Why Married People Are Happier, Healthier, and Better Off Financially* (New York: Doubleday, 2000), 2.

2. Arthur Levine and Jeanette S. Cureton, *When Hope and Fear Collide* (San Francisco: Jossey-Bass, 1998), 95.

3. Waite and Gallagher, *The Case for Marriage*, 2.

4. Genesis 2:18.

5. Genesis 2:24.

6. One exercise you and your dating partner can do together to measure your emotional intimacy is to rate the degree to which you feel each of these elements — love, respect, and appreciation — exists in your relationship. Rate each element on a scale of one to ten. Tell each other why your number was high or low. Give illustrations.

7. H. Weinstock et al. "Sexually transmitted diseases among American youth," *Perspectives on Sexual and Reproductive Health* 2004 (1): 6–10; cited in the Centers of Disease Control and Prevention report "Trends in Reportable Sexually Transmitted Diseases in the United States, 2006" at www.cdc.gov/std/stats/trends2006.htm.

8. Neil Howe and William Strauss, *Thirteenth GEN* (New York: Vintage Books, 1993), 148.

9. Glenn T. Stanton, *Why Marriage Matters* (Colorado Springs: Pinon, 1997), 34.

10. See 1 John 1:9.

11. Ephesians 4:15, 25.

12. Kim McAlister, "The X Generation," *HR Magazine*, May 1994, 21.

Chapter 12: *They're Not Just for Romantic Relationships*

1. Matthew 5:44.

CHAPTER 13: *Single with Kids*

1. Angie's story first appeared in Gary Chapman, *The Five Love Languages of Teenagers* (Chicago: Northfield, 2000), 217–18, from which it has been adapted.

2. Shmuel Shulman and Inge Seiffge-Krenke, *Fathers and Adolescents* (New York: Routledge, 1997), 97.

3. Gary Chapman and Ross Campbell, *The Five Love Languages of Children* (Chicago: Northfield, 1997), 173–74.

4. Sherill and Prudence Tippins, *Two of Us Make a World* (New York: Holt, 1995), 56.

5. You might want to use the following: Gary Chapman and Ross Campbell, "The Five Love Languages of Children Video Pack" (Nashville: Lifeway Christian Resources, 1998).

CHAPTER 14: *Success*

1. Tom Peters, *Thriving on Chaos: Handbook for a Management Revolution* (New York: Random House audio books, 1987).

2. Kevin Leman, *Winning the Rat Race Without Becoming a Rat* (Nashville: Nelson, 1996), 60, 99, 100.

3. Ibid., 100.

4. C. S. Lewis, *Mere Christianity* (New York: Macmillan, 1952), 116.

5. Matthew 5:43–44.

6. Matthew 5:45.

7. Romans 5:5.

8. Romans 5:8.

9. James S. Hewett, ed., *Illustrations Unlimited* (Wheaton, Ill.: Tyndale, 1988), 470.

10. For practical help, you may want to read Gary Chapman, *God Speaks Your Love Language* (Chicago: Northfield, 2009).

appendix:

THE FIVE LOVE LANGUAGES PROFILE

WORDS OF AFFIRMATION, quality time, gifts, acts of service, physical touch—which of these is your primary love language? You may already have an idea, or you may have no clue. "The Five Love Languages Profile" will help you know for sure.

The profile includes thirty pairs of statements. Read each pair and choose the one that better reflects your preferences. Then, in the right column, circle the letter that corresponds with the statement you choose. In some cases, you may wish that you could circle both, but you should choose only one to ensure the most accurate profile results.

When reading the profile statements, you'll see words like "special person" and "loved ones." When we think of love and love languages, our immediate thought may be of a romantic relationship. However, we express love and affection in a variety of contexts and relationships. As you work through the profile, think of a significant person with whom you are close: a boyfriend or girlfriend, a good friend, a parent, a colleague, etc.

Take the profile when you are relaxed and not pressed for time. After you've made your selections, go back and count the number of times you chose each letter. List the results in the appropriate spaces at the end of the profile. Then read "Interpreting and Using Your Profile Score," which follows the profile.

1.	I like to receive notes of affirmation.	A
	I like to be hugged.	E
2.	I like to spend one-to-one time with a person who is special to me.	B
	I feel loved when someone gives practical help to me.	D
3.	I like it when people give me gifts.	C
	I like leisurely visits with friends and loved ones.	B
4.	I feel loved when people do things to help me.	D
	I feel loved when people touch me.	E
5.	I feel loved when someone I love or admire puts his or her arm around me.	E
	I feel loved when I receive a gift from someone I love or admire.	C
6.	I like to go places with friends and loved ones.	B
	I like to high-five or hold hands with people who are special to me.	E
7.	Visible symbols of love (gifts) are very important to me.	C
	I feel loved when people affirm me.	A
8.	I like to sit close to people whom I enjoy being around.	E
	I like for people to tell me I am attractive/handsome.	A
9.	I like to spend time with friends and loved ones.	B
	I like to receive little gifts from friends and loved ones.	C
10.	Words of acceptance are important to me.	A
	I know someone loves me when he or she helps me.	D
11.	I like being together and doing things with friends and loved ones.	B
	I like it when kind words are spoken to me.	A
12.	What someone does affects me more than what he or she says.	D
	Hugs make me feel connected and valued.	E
13.	I value praise and try to avoid criticism.	A
	Several small gifts mean more to me than one large gift.	C

14. I feel close to someone when we are talking or doing something together. B

I feel closer to friends and loved ones when they touch me often. E

15. I like for people to compliment my achievements. A

I know people love me when they do things for me that they don't enjoy doing. D

16. I like to be touched as friends and loved ones walk by. E

I like it when people listen to me and show genuine interest in what I am saying. B

17. I feel loved when friends and loved ones help me with jobs or projects. D

I really enjoy receiving gifts from friends and loved ones. C

18. I like for people to compliment my appearance. A

I feel loved when people take time to understand my feelings. B

19. I feel secure when a special person is touching me. E

Acts of service make me feel loved. D

20. I appreciate the many things that special people do for me. D

I like receiving gifts that special people make for me. C

21. I really enjoy the feeling I get when someone gives me undivided attention. B

I really enjoy the feeling I get when someone does some act of service for me. D

22. I feel loved when a person celebrates my birthday with a gift. C

I feel loved when a person celebrates my birthday with meaningful words. A

23. I know a person is thinking of me when he or she gives me a gift. C

I feel loved when a person helps with my chores. D

24. I appreciate it when someone listens patiently and doesn't interrupt me. B

I appreciate it when someone remembers special days with a gift. C

25. I like knowing loved ones are concerned enough to help with my daily tasks. D

I enjoy extended trips with someone who is special to me. B

26. I enjoy kissing or being kissed by people with whom I am close. E

Receiving a gift given for no special reason excites me. C

27. I like to be told that I am appreciated. A

I like for a person to look at me when we are talking. B

28. Gifts from a friend or loved one are always special to me. C

I feel good when a friend or loved one touches me. E

29. I feel loved when a person enthusiastically does some task I have requested. D

I feel loved when I am told how much I am appreciated. A

30. I need to be touched every day.   E

     I need words of affirmation daily.   A

     TOTALS: A: _____ B: _____ C: _____ D: _____ E: _____

          A. Words of Affirmation   B. Quality Time   C. Receiving Gifts
                 D. Acts of Service   E. Physical Touch

INTERPRETING AND USING YOUR PROFILE SCORE

Which love language received the highest score? This is your primary love language. If point totals for two love languages are equal, you are "bilingual" and have two primary love languages. And, if you have a secondary love language, or one that is close in score to your primary love language, this means that both expressions of love are important to you. The highest possible score for any single love language is twelve.

Although you may have scored certain ones of the love languages more highly than others, try not to disregard those other languages as unimportant. Your friends and loved ones may express love in those ways, and it will pay great dividends for you to understand this about them. In the same way, it will benefit your friends and loved ones to know your love language and express their affection for you in ways that you interpret as love. Every time you or they speak one another's language, you score emotional points with one another. Of course, no one should be keeping a score sheet. The result of speaking a person's love language is more a feeling of "this person understands me and cares for me." Over time, this feeling multiplies into a stronger sense of connectedness.

Just as identifying and speaking a person's love language strengthens a relationship, not doing this can leave a friend or loved one feeling as if you do not love him or her. When people do not convey love in a way that is perceived as love, their efforts, though sincere, are somewhat wasted. This can be frustrating for both the giver of love and the intended recipient. You may have unknowingly been guilty of speaking a "foreign" love language in the past to someone you loved. Understanding the concept of love languages can help you know how to effectively express your feelings so that they are received and interpreted as you mean them to be.

If they've not already done so, encourage the special people in your life to take "The Five Love Languages Profile." Then discuss your respective love languages and use this insight to improve your relationships.

the five love languages — singles edition
STUDY GUIDE

INTRODUCTION

We are about to experience a journey of discovery as we search for under-standing regarding one of life's greatest challenges: *How can we fulfill our need to give and receive emotional love as singles?*

The guide for navigating this journey is a format we call C-groups. C-groups are a simple and extremely practical technique for living out the principles shared in *The Five Love Languages Singles Edition*. Much easier than a traditional small group, you can use C-groups in a home, a workplace setting, a church-based group, or even adapt it to fit a weekend retreat format.

Depending on your time and limitations, each session can be shared over a 30-60 minute breakfast, lunch, or evening meal time. Of course, the material is also usable for personal study and reflection, though maxi-mum impact will only be achieved in shared community.

Before starting, be sure each group member has a copy of *The Five Love Languages Singles Edition*. In each of the fourteen interactive sessions, Gary Chapman leads us through the four steps of a C-group:

CHECK PROGRESS: Each session begins by having each person share what has happened in their lives since the previous C-group. Before learning anything new, check how previous information has been experienced in one another's lives.

CONSIDER THE TRUTH: Next, interact with one another using the study guide questions based on each chapter of *The Five Love Languages Singles Edition*. Allow each person to share what has made the biggest impact in their life or thinking.

CONNECT WITH YOUR LIFE: Third, each session is designed to advance life-change in its readers. This includes journaling points and specific action steps you can apply during the next week to encourage use of the concepts in everyday life situations.

COMMUNICATE TO OTHERS: Ultimately, you must pass on what you are learning to others. The most direct way to accomplish this is to facilitate a C-group of your own.

Here's how this group works. At your first gathering, meet with your friends and bring your copy of *The Five Love Languages Singles Edition* book. This guide will walk you through each step of the process. There is no outside preparation needed.

Once your C-group has begun, members can (and should be encouraged to) begin additional groups where they not only live out the five love languages, but also communicate the concepts they have learned with others.

Can it be this easy? While no group is without its problems, sharing what you are personally gaining from *The Five Love Languages Singles Edition* will create shared experiences that become memories and foundations for a lifetime of better relationships. So hang on and prepare for a life-changing ride that will radically alter your view of life!

SESSION 1

SINGLE ADULTS: *Significant And Growing*

Check Progress

• What was your primary reason for joining this group?

• What concerns do you have as you embark on an enhanced understanding of love as a single adult?

Consider the Truth

• Of the five groups of singles mentioned in chapter 1, which category best describes you? (never married, divorced, separated but not divorced, widowed, or single parent)

• During a time of need, how have you experienced a friend's love similar to Rob's story (p. 17–18)? What difference did it make in your life?

• How strongly do you agree or disagree with the author's quote that, "Much of the pain in broken relationships in our world stems from the truth that many of us in Western culture have never been serious students of love"? (p. 20). Why did you choose this particular response?

• What idea or story in chapter 1 has made the biggest impact in your attitude about love?

Connect with Your Life

• Chapter 1 describes love as a "learned emotion." What is something specific you could do this week to become a better student in showing love to others?

• *Journaling Point:* Take some time this week to list people who have shown significant love toward you during your lifetime. What common themes can you identify from your list?

- *Action Point:* Write or call one person from your journal list to thank him or her for the difference this love made to you.

Communicate to Others

- How do you feel about the challenge to start a group like this with others? If you were to begin your own group at some point, who would you want to involve?

SESSION 2

THIS IS IT: *The Key to Your Relationships*

Check Progress

- How have you connected the previous session's learning with your life since our last meeting?
- Share highlights from your journaling and action points from last week.

Consider the Truth

- Chapter 2 shares: "All your relationships spring from the relationship with your parents" (p. 24). How have you seen this to be true in your life?
- We often believe love is simply something that "happens to you." In what ways is this true? In what ways is this not true?
- The major focus in chapter 2 argues for two stages of romantic love: obsessive and covenant. What are some differences between these two stages you have experienced during a relationship?
- The author explains that the five love languages apply to all relationships. What are some areas outside of a dating relationship where you see a need for applying the five love languages?

NOTES

Connect with Your Life

- Ask a friend who is currently in a dating relationship how the relationship is going. Use what you have learned to decide if the couple is primarily in the obsessive or covenant love stage or a combination of both.

- *Journaling Point:* Use at least one page to write your response to the following statement: "The way my parents (or other guardian) expressed love to me has affected my attitude toward others by

_____.

- *Action Point:* Contact one of your parents this week (if applicable) and share something that you have learned from this week's session.

Communicate to Others

- Have you shared your learning from session one with anyone since last week? What happened? Who do you know who could use a copy of *The Five Love Languages Singles Edition* right now?

SESSION 3

LOVE LANGUAGE #1: *Words Of Affirmation*

Check Progress

- What is one observation you have noticed in the past week regarding how your style of showing love is the same or different from your parents?

- If you have communicated with a parent since last time, what happened? What was his or her response to what you shared from your learning?

NOTES

_____
_____
_____
_____
_____
_____
_____
_____
_____
_____
_____
_____
_____
_____
_____
_____
_____
_____
_____
_____
_____
_____
_____
_____
_____
_____
_____
_____
_____
_____
_____

Consider the Truth:

- What was your response to the statement that words of affirmation "can be learned" (p. 36)? How have you seen this to be true or untrue in your conversations with others?

- How does Brian's story connect with what you have encountered in dating relationships (pp. 37–38)? What problems do you run into when "it gets personal"?

- The author encourages us to "start where we are" in affirming others. If you were to evaluate yourself from 1 to 10 on how affirming you are, what would you say? Where are you "starting from" in your ability to affirm other people?

- Review the dialects of affirming words (encouragement, praise, kind words). Which dialect(s) do you see as your strongest? Your weakest? Who in your group do you see as a champion in one of these three dialects?

Connect with Your Life

- Collect affirming words others have shared with you.

- These could include notes, e-mails, work reviews, Christmas cards, or even verbal comments that you write down. Ask, "What made these words so meaningful?"

- *Journaling Point:* As Brian was encouraged (p. 46), make a list of potential affirmations you could share with those in your life. Use the following categories as a starting point: 1) parents, 2) siblings 3) coworkers 4) close friends 5) dating relationship.

- *Action Point:* Write an affirming handwritten note to someone in your group today, preferably before your group time ends. Specifically consider how to include the dialects of encouragement, praise, and kind words as you write.

NOTES

Communicate to Others

- Affirm someone in your workplace or other setting today. Explain to them how *The Five Love Languages Singles Edition* has helped you in showing encouragement. Offer to share more about this helpful resource with them. Even better: Invite them to your next group meeting if it is an open group.

SESSION 4

LOVE LANGUAGE #2: *Gifts*

Check Progress

- What has happened since your last meeting as you intentionally affirmed others in your life?

- As you reflected on how others have affirmed you in the past, what did you discover as some of the reasons their words were so meaningful?

Consider the Truth

- Review the story of the widow's chair (pp.57-58). What is one of the greatest gifts you have ever been given? What made it special from other gifts?

- Using the example of the wedding ring, the author teaches that the emotional love associated with the gift is more important that the gift itself (p. 59). How have you seen this to be true with gifts you have received? How has it been untrue?

- This session shows there is a language to gift giving. Review these areas (pp. 60–63). What is most important to you when you receive a gift?

- What was your first response to Bridget's teddy bears (p. 66)? What "teddy bear" equivalents do you see in the other people around you? In your life?

NOTES

_____
_____
_____
_____
_____
_____
_____
_____
_____
_____
_____
_____
_____
_____
_____
_____
_____
_____
_____
_____
_____
_____
_____
_____
_____
_____
_____
_____
_____
_____
_____
_____
_____
_____
_____
_____
_____

Connect with Your Life

• *Journaling Point:* Money is often the number one barrier to expressing the love language of gift-giving (p. 63). Write your answer to: "What are my beliefs about giving gifts?" You may be surprised at your answers, but the result will show where you can better improve in speaking this love language.

• *Action Point:* Who is a person in your life who clearly responds to the language of gift-giving? Purchase or create a gift for them this week. Pay special attention to how they respond to this gift.

Communicate to Others

• If you start giving small gifts to people this week, someone will likely ask, "Why?" Tell them it is the result of a book you have been reading lately. Offer to share a copy with them. Even better, buy them a copy as a gift.

SESSION 5

LOVE LANGUAGE #3: *Acts of Service*

Check Progress

• What was the result of your gift-giving experience since the last meeting?

• As you wrote about your view toward money as a gift-giving barrier, what unique insights emerged?

Consider the Truth

• Review Jenny's story on page 73. Who in your life who has spoken acts of service to you recently? What made it stand out as a special gift?

• Acts of service is a love language spanning a vast variety of options. What are

NOTES

some of the ways you commonly see others performing acts of service?

• Leah's primary love language was acts of service (pp. 78-81). How have you seen acts of service stand out in your dating relationships? Have you ever dated someone whose primary love language was acts of service? What was it like?

• The author wraps up this chapter saying, "When we learn to speak each other's love language early in our relationships, we are able to keep each other's love tanks full" (p. 84). How have you experienced this in your past or current relationships?

Connect with Your Life

• Consider your circle of relationships. Who responds the most to acts of service? What specific factors caused you to decide on these people?

• *Journaling Point:* Write your answer to: "How easily do I show acts of service to others?" List at least five past examples. What common elements exist? How can this knowledge help you improve in this area?

• *Action Point:* Perform acts of service for at least three friends this week and watch how they respond. Who appears to respond the most to this love anguage? How can these observations be helpful in your dating relationships?

Communicate to Others

• When someone responds to an act of service you do this week, say, "This is part of what I am learning in building better relationships. I would love to share more about this with you." Share a copy of this study or *The Five Love Languages Singles Edition* to those interested.

NOTES

SESSION 6

LOVE LANGUAGE #4: *Quality Time*

Check Progress

• What happened when you showed acts of service to others since last week? Consider sharing both your highs and lows from this learning experience.

• Who are some people you identified whose primary love language is acts of service? How has this practice helped you identify the love languages of others?

Consider the Truth

• Mike's story on page 87 reveals his need for quality time. When is a time you have been frustrated in a relationship due to lack of close times together?

• "The important thing about a mother rolling the ball to her two-year-old is not the activity itself, but the emotions that are created between the mother and her child" (p. 88). How have you seen this to be true in your relationship experiences?

• Reflect on the dialects of quality time (conversations, listening, activities). Which dialect is most important to you personally? Where do you see the greatest need for improvement in your relationships with others?

• Pages 96 and 97 discuss the importance of creating memories. What are some specific ways you could create positive memories in a dating relationship? Make a group list to combine your best ideas.

Connect with Your Life

• *Journaling Point:* Write down at least five of your favorite childhood memories. What factors made these times meaningful over other memories? How could these same factors be helpful in your current and future relationships?

NOTES

• *Action Point:* Choose a dialect (conversations, listening, activities). Try one out with a friend or significant other this week, specifically applying the ideas shared in the book. Be prepared to share what happened at your next meeting.

Communicate to Others

• People are constantly looking for ways to have more quality time in their life. When the topic comes up, share what you have learned this week. Offer to spend quality time in conversation with them about *The Five Love Languages Singles Edition* or in starting a group like this one.

SESSION 7

LOVE LANGUAGE #5: *Physical Touch*

Check Progress:

• Share your struggles and successes from your attempts at expressing quality time since your last meeting. What was the most significant result of your personal applications?

• What were some of your special childhood memories from your journaling last week? How did this process help you in observing the value of quality time?

Consider the Truth:

• "It's funny that no one hesitates to touch a baby. . . but here I sit sometimes dying to have someone touch me and no one does" (p. 99). How do you feel about this woman's statement? Why do you think this is the case for so many people?

• Review the different kinds of touches on pages 101–103. What are some of the concerns you have about approaching the issue of physical touch with others?

NOTES

- Marti describes herself as not being a "touchy-feely" person (p. 107). The author challenges her to learn physical touch by "trying." How do you feel about the idea of "learning" to touch?

- Timing, setting, and manner of touching are each described as important aspects of the touching process. Look at the descriptions of these areas and share which area you consider of greatest importance (pp. 110-112). Why do you feel this way?

Connect with Your Life:

- Can you think of a friend or family member whose primary love language is physical touch? What specific actions helped you decide on this person? How could this knowledge help you better express quality touch toward others?

- *Journaling Point:* Inappropriate touch is perhaps the most difficult subject to discuss in a group setting. Write in your journal your thoughts on inappropriate touch, whether a personal experience or one you are aware of from another person. Consider not only the event itself but also why it has had such a long-term impact. If this area surfaces deep emotional response, it may be wise to seek additional help from a close friend or counselor.

- *Action Point*: Learn by "trying." Select a trusted friend, family member, or dating relationship and experiment with physical touch in a new way such as hugging a brother you usually do not embrace. Pay special attention to the response by both you and the other person. Be prepared to share your observations the next time the group meets.

Communicate to Others:

- If someone asks you why you are suddenly a "hugger" or seem to be reaching out more, share what you are learning. This

NOTES

could be a great opportunity to begin gathering friends or coworkers for a new C-group that you can lead.

SESSION 8

YOU GO FIRST: *Discovering Your Primary Love Language*

Check Progress

• What happened when you hugged someone new last week? How did you feel after the experience?

• If you asked a high-touch person this week about their primary love language of touch, what response did you receive?

Consider the Truth

• Based on your behavior, what do you think others would say your primary love language is? Why would they choose that particular response?

• See the *Love Language Profile* in the appendix. If you have completed it, what were your results? How surprised were you by these results?

• What do you think are the most important ways to discover the love languages of others? How good do you think you would be at determining the primary love language of the members of your group?

• The author also shares the concept of experimenting to discover a person's love language. Since you have likely done this as a result of earlier sessions, describe what has helped you best determine the primary love language of others.

Connect with Your Life

• *Journaling Point*: Answer the question: "What is my primary love language?" After writing your response, spend at least one page explaining why you

NOTES

selected that choice. If you have trouble determining only one area, what common elements stand out in both areas you selected?

• *Action Point:* Select someone you know closely and seek to determine his or her primary love language. After you have decided, share the concept of the love languages with them and ask if they agree with your observation. Consider how quickly you were able to decide and what factors helped you come to this conclusion.

Communicate to Others

• Share the concept of the five love languages with someone this week. If they are responsive to the concept, offer to meet with them (and possibly a couple of other friends) to talk more about it. This can act as a "preview" for a future C-group.

SESSION 9

FAMILY: *Connect the Dots with Your Immediate Family*

Check Progress

• How does it feel to live a week knowing your personal love language? In what specific ways has this knowledge changed your daily life?

• Who did you discuss the five love languages with this week? What was his or her response?

Consider the Truth

• Susan discovered the power of love languages maximized within her own family (p. 129). What is an example of how you have experienced the love languages with a parent or sibling in the past?

NOTES

• After some difficult experiences, Jennifer began speaking the primary love languages of her parents when she communicated with them (pp. 135-136). Though difficult to initiate, the change proved extremely effective. In what specific ways could you better speak the love language of one of your family members?

• If applicable, share about your siblings with your group members. What are their love languages? How are they different from yours?

Connect with Your Life

• *Journaling Point:* Complete the chart on page 146, either in the book or in your journal. Commit to action with at least one family member before your next session.

• *Action Point:* After selecting the family member to share with, specifically communicate at least one time using what you believe is their primary love language. Closely observe what happens. Be prepared to share with your group.

Communicate to Others

• At least one family member should be curious about the five love languages by the time you apply the information from this chapter. Tell them more about what you are learning. Consider starting a "distance-based" C-group with your parents or siblings, using this material and the book as a learning tool to enhance your family relationships.

NOTES

SESSION 10

DATING RELATIONSHIPS—PART 1:
Love Languages And Your Special Someone

Check Progress

• What action step did you make toward a family member since last week? What happened?

• How has discovering the love languages of your family members impacted your attitude toward them?

Consider the Truth

• Have you ever given up on dating? What factors caused you to make this decision?

• This chapter lists five reasons for why we date (pp. 148–154). Which areas do you consider to be most important? How have you sometimes felt you have "failed" dating due to unclear objectives in one of these areas?

• A major reason for dating is to discover the kind of person we will marry (p. 153). How have your past dating relationships helped you better see what you want in the person you will marry?

• Shelley and Neil felt the excitement had left their relationship (p. 155). How have you experienced this issue in a dating relationship? How would knowing the five love languages have helped you?

Connect with Your Life

• *Journaling Point:* Choose a past dating relationship and write your response to the following: "The discoveries I made about myself during this relationship were. . . . The discoveries I made about the person I want to marry were. . . ."

• *Action Point:* If you are in a current dating relationship, intentionally invest time to

NOTES

_____

_____

_____

_____

_____

_____

_____

_____

_____

_____

_____

_____

_____

_____

_____

_____

_____

_____

_____

_____

_____

_____

_____

_____

_____

_____

_____

_____

_____

_____

_____

_____

_____

_____

_____

_____

learn the personality, personal beliefs, and primary love language of the other person through active listening. If you are not currently in a dating relationship, begin changing by developing a wholesome relationship with a single person of the opposite sex (p. 148).

Communicate to Others

• Who else do you know who would be helped through the information in this session? Why not share what you have been learning with them, encouraging this person with a copy of this book?

SESSION 11

DATING RELATIONSHIPS—PART 2:
Should Love Lead to Marriage?

Check Progress

• What was the most significant moment in your past week as a result of learning about the five love languages?

• Share discoveries from your journaling time and action steps from last week.

Consider the Truth

• Mark and Sylvia struggled with a lack of emotional love in their marriage (p. 162). What concerns do you have about the loss of emotional love in your future marriage?

• Glance at the seven common purposes of love on page 167. Which reasons do you think people consider most important when they think about marriage?

• Marital unity serves as the deeper purpose for marriage. Of the different areas of unity (intellectual, social, emotional, spiritual, physical), which do you consider to be the easiest to develop in a future marriage? The most difficult? Why?

- What do you consider as the most important aspects of spiritual unity in a marriage relationship (p. 173)? How have you seen this to be true even within dating relationships?

Connect with Your Life

- *Journaling Point:* Past scars are painful and often extremely difficult to discuss. Consider journaling to process past hurts, deciding to "deal with it" rather than ignore problems. If you discover overwhelming issues through this process, consider talking with a trusted friend or counselor who can encourage you in this area.

- *Action Point:* Talk to a friend who is married. Ask them how their marriage has helped fulfill their desire for unity. Gather all the information you can. Without sharing information that is too personal, be prepared to relate your findings to other group members next week.

Communicate to Others

- Who do you know right now who is currently considering marriage? Share this material with them, doing so in a way that comes across as you seeking advice from them. If they are open to it, share a copy of *The Five Love Languages Singles Edition* with them. Who knows what it could do to also help your friend in his or her road toward married life?

SESSION 12

THEY'RE NOT JUST FOR ROMANTIC RELATIONSHIPS: *Roommates, Classmates And Coworkers*

Check Progress

- Share findings from your discussion with a married friend since last week. What were the biggest surprises?

NOTES

244

• Who have you shared your copy of *The Five Love Languages Singles Edition* with since last time?

Consider the Truth

• Reed struggled with a messy roommate (pp. 179–182). What is a roommate struggle you have encountered in the past? How could you have responded differently with what you now know about the five love languages?

• This chapter suggests the five love languages are applicable to all human relationships. What is one way you have seen the five love languages illustrated in the life of someone close to your life now, whether roommate, classmate, or coworker?

• "Singles have few friends but many acquaintances" (see p. 186). How do you feel about this statement? How can using your primary love language help you in serving others?

• The author provides several examples of communicating according to the love languages of those around us (pp. 187–192). Which of these examples connected most strongly with you? Why?

Connect with Your Life

• *Journaling Point:* Make a list of the closest five to ten people in your life right now outside of your immediate family. Choose three of these people and list a specific way you can serve them based on their primary love language.

• *Action Point:* Create your own serving story. Choose your roommate, a classmate, or coworker and serve them in one specific way this week using their primary love language. Be prepared to share what happened with your group next time.

NOTES

Communicate to Others

• Since we are discussing roommates, classmates, and coworkers, chose a person in one of these areas and share this chapter with them. Consider starting a C-group with them within the next two weeks.

SESSION 13

SINGLE WITH KIDS: *Love Languages and Single Parents*

Check Progress

• What happened when you served your roommate, classmate, or coworker according to his or her primary love language?

• How are you feeling about beginning a new C-group? What kind of impact could your group have if each of you were involved in helping a few other friends experience what you have learned recently?

Consider the Truth

• How would you feel if you were in Angie's situation (pp. 195–196)? If you have any single parents in your group, encourage them to share their unique perspective in this area. As an alternative, share a story of a single parent you know and how their life has affected you.

• In what ways would expressing the five love languages with children be different than with adults? If you have attempted to do this recently, what has been your experience?

• What was discipline like for you as a child? What would you desire to keep the same in disciplining your own children? What would you desire to do differently?

NOTES

_____
_____
_____
_____
_____
_____
_____
_____
_____
_____
_____
_____
_____
_____
_____
_____
_____
_____
_____
_____
_____
_____
_____
_____
_____
_____
_____
_____
_____
_____
_____
_____

• The author expresses the importance for single parents to also meet their own need for love (pp. 204–205). If you are a single parent, what has best helped you in this area? If you were raised in a single parent family, what helped your parent most meeting their own need for love?

Connect with Your Life

• *Journaling Point:* List some single parents you know personally. What could you do to help one of these parents in a specific way this week?

• *Action Point:* If possible, informally interview a single parent. Ask what has been most helpful and most difficult both as an individual and in the role of parent. Seek understanding that would be helpful for you or to share with your group.

• Action Point: If you are a single parent, evaluate how well you are meeting your own need for love. As you encounter a weak area, search for a positive option to improve your situation. Remember, if your love needs are met, you can better meet the love needs of your child or children.

Communicate to Others

• Only one more week to go! If you have not already done so, actively seek at least two other people you can meet with in your own C-group. One great way to do this is to join with another person in your current group to co-lead a new group. This will create more confidence and provide help for one another along the way.

NOTES

_____

_____

_____

_____

_____

_____

_____

_____

_____

_____

_____

_____

_____

_____

_____

_____

_____

_____

_____

_____

_____

_____

_____

_____

_____

_____

_____

SESSION 14

SUCCESS: *Love Is the Key*

Check Progress

• What connections did you have with single parents within the past week? What happened?

• If your action step was to help a single parent, what was the result? If you are a single parent, what changes have you seen in your life since last week?

Consider the Truth

• "Success is making the most of what you are with what you've got" (p. 207). How strongly do you agree or disagree with this definition? How would you define success?

• Loving people is prescribed in this chapter as the key to successful business and personal relationships. How have you seen this to be true in a recent professional situation? A personal relationship experience?

• The author recommends that you ignore your feelings in showing love to someone you don't necessarily like (p. 212). How does this advice contrast what we usually believe about love? Does this practice seem hypocritical to you? Why or why not?

• Review the story of Mr. Anderson's young worker on pages 213–214. How could you use his focus on evaluation in your work life? In your personal life?

Connect with Your Life

• *Journaling Point:* Write down your major roles in life (such as family member or employee) and list what you would consider success in each area. What would it take to reach this level?

NOTES

NOTES

- *Action Point:* Since this is your last week together, take some time to evaluate how this group has impacted your life. Describe your "before" and "after" situation. What will be the most important lesson you have learned that you will use on an ongoing basis?

- *Celebrate:* Schedule a time to celebrate the completion of your group! This can be during this same time, a meal at someone's home or another social outing of your choosing.

Communicate to Others

What now? Armed with the tools from this book, you are now responsible to utilize these abilities to their greatest advantage. If you have not decided to start another group with this material, commit right now to help others learn what you have gained. Second, regularly communicate using the love languages of others, changing lives and becoming more successful along the way. Finally, consider a deeper spiritual commitment to the Creator of love and the One who is love. The greater your spiritual relationship, the greater you can show the five languages within your other relationships in life.

THINGS I WISH I'D KNOWN
BEFORE WE GOT MARRIED

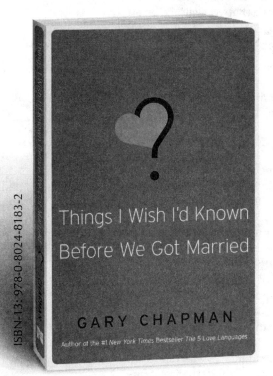

This is not a book simply to be read. It is a book to be experienced. The material lends itself to heart-felt discussions by dating or engaged couples. To jump-start the exchanges, each short chapter includes insightful "Talking it Over" questions and suggestions. And, the book includes information on interactive websites as well as books that will enhance the couples experience.

NORTHFIELD
PUBLISHING

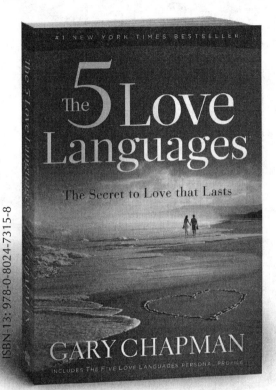

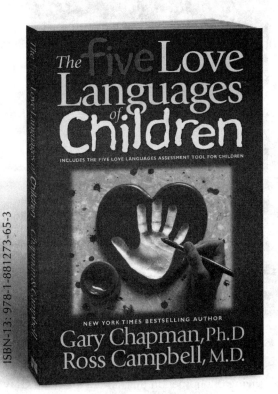

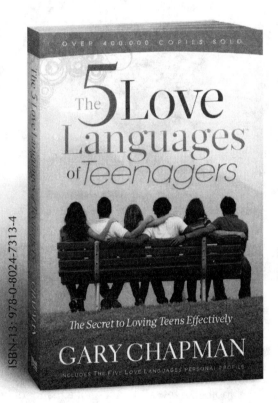

THE FIVE LANGUAGES OF APOLOGY

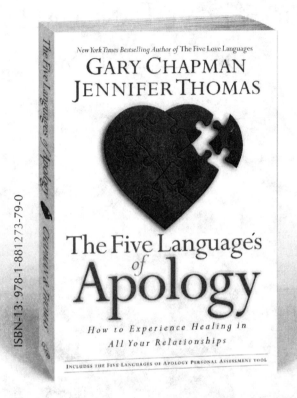

ISBN-13: 978-1-881273-79-0

Just as you have a distinct love language, you also hear and express the words and gestures of apology in a different language. This groundbreaking study of the way we apologize reveals that it's not a matter of will—it's a matter of how. By helping you identify the languages of apology, this book clears the way toward healing and sustaining vital relationships.

5LOVELANGUAGES.COM • MOODYPUBLISHERS.COM

ANGER

We live in an angry society.
You can't escape it.
But this candid look at a volatile human emotion can
help you deal with it productively.

THE MARRIAGE YOU'VE ALWAYS WANTED

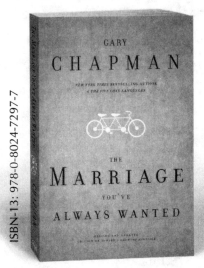

ISBN-13: 978-0-8024-7297-7

It's never too late to begin enjoying your ideal marriage. And it's never too early to improve your relationship. This thorough, easy-to-follow guide gives you the blueprint for an emotionally fulfilling marriage that is well within your reach.

THE MARRIAGE YOU'VE ALWAYS WANTED
BIBLE STUDY

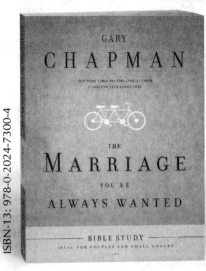

ISBN-13: 978-0-2024-7300-4

From the *New York Times* bestselling author and international speaker comes this interactive, practical resource designed to help couples grow closer to each other and closer to God. Couples will discuss and reflect on such areas as money, anger, forgiveness, and spirituality. Perfect for couples and small groups!

NORTHFIELD
PUBLISHING

5LOVELANGUAGES.COM • MOODYPUBLISHERS.COM